Finding Courage to Let YOU Out!

Living Our Human-NESS
with Our Human MESS

Dr. Natacha D. Nelson D.C, M.A.

BALBOA.
PRESS
A DIVISION OF HAY HOUSE

Balboa Press books may be ordered through booksellers or by contacting:

Balboa Press
A Division of Hay House
1663 Liberty Drive
Bloomington, IN 47403
www.balboapress.com
1 (877) 407-4847

Because of the dynamic nature of the Internet, any web addresses or links contained in this book may have changed since publication and may no longer be valid. The views expressed in this work are solely those of the author and do not necessarily reflect the views of the publisher, and the publisher hereby disclaims any responsibility for them.

The author of this book does not dispense medical advice or prescribe the use of any technique as a form of treatment for physical, emotional, or medical problems without the advice of a physician, either directly or indirectly. The intent of the author is only to offer information of a general nature to help you in your quest for emotional and spiritual well-being. In the event you use any of the information in this book for yourself, which is your constitutional right, the author and the publisher assume no responsibility for your actions.

Any people depicted in stock imagery provided by Getty Images are models, and such images are being used for illustrative purposes only. Certain stock imagery © Getty Images.

Print information available on the last page.

ISBN: 978-1-9822-1869-0 (sc)
ISBN: 978-1-9822-1868-3 (hc)
ISBN: 978-1-9822-1873-7 (e)

Library of Congress Control Number: 2018914834

Balboa Press rev. date: 01/11/2019

Dedication

This book is dedicated to the little girl who forgot just how loveable she really is:

and to this little girl, that she never forgets:

Acknowledgements

To my mom, Arlette. Who's fierce, defiant spirit infuses in me the strength to always get back up, no matter what, and find a way to fight.

To my father, Darnel. Who's rebellious nature propels me to challenge the standard beliefs.

To my grandmother, Jeanne. Who's enduring nightingale spirit extends my wings farther and higher than I thought possible.

To my daughter, Jasmine. Who's playful spirit reconnected me with Life's magic, igniting me with the courage to fly.

To my Enduring friendships, regardless of space and time: Stefany, Jennifer and Amanda

To the many, many people I have met on this journey, Seth, Linda, Monique, Kimberly, Guy, Brittany, Marco, Colette, France, Patricia, Christine, Isabelle, Eric, Bruno, Annick, Lovie, Trinette, Steve, Tristin.

Special thank you to the Beach Volleyball Supporting cast of Characters, for your continued friendship, laughter and competitive spirits that kept me afloat.

To the patients/ clients, you trusted me with your physical health, your emotional wellness and the opportunity for me to uncover my unique gifts as a healer.

To my USM Family, for offering me the safe, loving space to explore the depths of my Soul.

PART 1

Chapter 1

"Why do I have to go? Why are you sending me away? I want to stay here and be with you. Please, Mom, don't make me go."

My lopsided, sagging braids mirrored the feelings in my heart. Holding my mom's hand while walking through the international terminal at the San Francisco airport, thoughts swirled through my head as I hopelessly wondered how to change her mind.

I was eleven years old and not sure how to get my mom's attention to tell her how scared I was, to let her know how terrified I felt to speak up. Honestly, I did not want to spend the summer in Europe with her friends—friends I didn't remember ever meeting. Being with our distant family without her, without Grandmommy, seemed cruel. Heartbroken and discouraged, I gave up trying and accepted that I would not see her for eleven weeks.

At the gate, the ticketing agent put a blue, white, and red plastic pouch around my shoulders. It's the unmistakable announcement to the flight staff and other passengers that I was a minor traveling alone and that strangers should help me if I became lost. I didn't want strangers to look at me or to help me. I didn't want to be alone. This was not how flying was supposed to be.

I was supposed to be sandwiched between my grandmother, Jeanne, and my mom, Arlette. This was how each of the dozen previous flights to France and Germany were.

I knew Mom loved me. I wished I knew why she was sending me away. An entire summer without her and my friends, and without the comforts of my room. I knew I should not ask why. Asking that would indicate that I was scared and questioning her decision. Neither was allowed in our home, according to Mom. Showing any emotions, especially in public, was unacceptable and forbidden.

At eleven years old, I was tall enough to stand eye to eye with my mom, but I dared not look into her eyes. I was grateful for my physical stature, as I attempted to appear older than my age. I carried my head high, shoulders back, and chin up, desperately attempting to convey the courage, confidence, and strength missing just below my skin's surface.

I hugged Mom while mining deep for the highest level of false bravado I could achieve. Using all of my might, my full-toothed smile took over. My smile veiled my quivering lips. I willed my eyelids to stay open while tilting my head slightly back. My warm, unseen tears slid down the back of my throat.

I did it. There was not even a sniffle as Mom and I parted. My wobbly knees buckled beneath the heavy burden of hurt and despair lodged in my throat. When I reached my assigned seat, the overwhelming emotional toll forced my legs to collapse. Crumpling, my body followed.

It took the entire flight, eleven hours, to regain my composure, to retrieve my energy reserves to face what awaited in Dusseldorf. I hoped the daughters would be nice to me. I wondered if they spoke English. Or maybe French? Maybe Mom told me, but I felt too betrayed by her to pay attention as she explained the details. Completely shocked, I was only informed a few days ago about this trip.

Feeling abandoned after her sudden announcement on my last day of seventh grade, I wondered what other secrets she was keeping from me. Was this trip really only eleven weeks? Or would it be longer, maybe permanent? What else was she not telling me? I never knew what was in her mind. She only shared with me what

I needed to know, when I needed to know it, leaving me to follow her directions.

Besides, my ideas were dumb. Nothing I had to say was important. I guess I was not old enough to have ideas that mattered. So much for spending the summer with Suzie, my new best friend. My plans with her were overlooked.

When the food cart came down the aisle, I was so hungry. I knew that if I asked, the flight attendant would give me extra. They always did. Maybe because I was a kid. Maybe my dimples and my big, brave smile were irresistible. Or maybe they felt sorry for me too. This time, I was flying alone. She would definitely give me more. She gave me an entire bag containing one hundred miniature servings of peanuts, an entire can of orange soda, and an extra one to keep for the movie. I was going to be okay.

In a calmed, dreamy state, my mind drifted to eighteen months earlier.

Chapter 2

"I'll be taking Grandmommy to the doctor today, then I will pick you up from school."

As I ran to catch the bus, I said, "Okay. Bye."

It was rare for Mom to pick me up from school. Normally, Grandmommy waited for me at the bus stop, and then Mom came home much later, after Grandmommy and I had dinner. Dinner was just with my mom that night.

"Grandmommy is staying at the doctor's tonight," she said as we ate. "I will bring her home tomorrow."

"She's okay, right?" I asked.

"Yes. Nothing's wrong. My friend Ingrid is coming tomorrow from Germany. Just for a little while. She wants to visit California. She'll be staying in the other room, so please take your toys out and make room for her."

An eerie stillness hovered over the house; I missed the sound of *Wonder Woman* playing in the background. It was Grandmommy's favorite television show. Watching Linda Carter spin into character to save the planet always made her giggle. The night didn't feel the same. I was supposed to be in her bed to snuggle myself to sleep. I would put my cold feet on her, and she would squeal, pretending to push me out. But I wouldn't leave, and she wouldn't make me. Once her electric blanket got as hot as she liked, I would leave to my bed.

That night, I just went straight to my room after I cleaned up. I was too sad to be with Mom. She seemed sad too. I thought she wanted to be left alone. She didn't ask me to come in, so I didn't want to bother her.

There was no smell of breakfast the next morning when I woke. Oh, yeah. Grandmommy was at the doctor's office. At least she would be back that night. The house felt weird without her. There was a void.

"You can take the bus home today," Mom said. "Ingrid is here from Germany, and I'm checking on Grandmommy today."

Ingrid greeted me at the bus stop. Grandmommy must be too tired to walk the few blocks. I couldn't wait to see her. Mom was home too. *How fun that everyone is home*, I thought.

"Come sit over here with us," Mom whispered.

I looked around but didn't see Grandmommy.

Mom said, "I took Grandmommy to the hospital yesterday so the doctors could help her. They were not able to help. She died this afternoon."

Silent and limp, I fell into Mom's arms. Despite the swell of tears, I didn't cry. I was angry and felt confused. I felt numb.

I didn't know Grandmommy was sick. She seemed fine to me. No one told me she was sick. I didn't get to say goodbye. Mom lied to me. She lied to me. I couldn't believe she would lie to me. Why would she keep this kind of secret from me? I didn't know I wasn't going to see her again. She didn't even take me to the hospital. How come she wouldn't let me see her? I hated her for keeping this a secret from me. Grandmommy was gone, and I didn't get to hug her or say goodbye.

I fell asleep while thinking, *Grandmommy died today. Grandmommy died today. Grandmommy died today.* I wished I could get up and take the needle off the scratched vinyl to make the unacceptable voice in my mind stop. I wanted to stay awake until my mom came in. I wanted her to hug me. I wanted to cry. I was not sure if it was okay for me to cry, at least not in front of her. Maybe it was best if she didn't come in so I could cry.

I woke up to the smell of breakfast cooking. It was all a nightmare, I thought; Grandmommy was alive. I rushed into the kitchen, but my heart fell, seeing Ingrid's beautiful breakfast on the table. The nightmare was real. I could not cry. I could not make her feel bad. I didn't want Mom to see me cry. I knew seeing me cry made her feel bad.

Taking a bite of the Nutella on toast crushed my heart. This was what Grandmommy always had waiting for me after school. I would never get to have this snack with her again. Waiting for my mom, who had not come down from her room yet, I ate another grilled toast with Nutella. Then another. By the third piece, my stomach felt stretched to its limit, but I ate a fourth. In my stomach, it was as if the bread soaked up all of my swallowed tears. With an aching stomach, I went back to my room. Hoping Mom would come comfort me before school, I deliberately took longer to get ready, in case she needed extra time to find the right words for me.

I heard Mom in the kitchen with Ingrid. Realizing she was not going to open the door to my bedroom, I came out on my own. Mom was crying at the counter; I let her know I was ready for school, making no mention of her ignoring my silent pleas for her comfort. Peering at Mom, I wondered why she didn't come into my room to comfort me, to talk with me. I desperately needed her to tell me what would happen next. Would there be a funeral? What would that be like? Would I see Grandmommy's dead body? I was not sure if I wanted to or not. I hoped I was not too scared. I had never seen a dead body before. TV didn't count; it's not real. Who would take me to the bus stop? Who would be waiting for me after school? What would happen to me? Would I be sent to live somewhere else? So many questions I needed answers to, in order to feel safe. Terror rose in my body; I was uncertain of what life was going to look like now. Would I be separated from my mom?

"Do your best in school today," she said. "I know it is hard. But I know you will be okay. Just be brave. Ingrid will be here this afternoon."

Go to school? I had to go to school?! How was I supposed to go to school? What was I supposed to say? Did I just act the same, as if nothing happened? I didn't know what I was supposed to do. How was I supposed to act? It was probably best if I said nothing. As long as I didn't cry or act sad, no one would know. No one would ask. I would just try to focus at school until Mom told me what to do. Until she told me what would happen next, I would just stay quiet and not ask. For now, no one needed to know.

Until she told me what to do, I would fix myself my favorite snack: toasted bread with Nutella. Two pieces with extra Nutella melting in the crevices. Just how Grandmommy would have made for me. I can imagine her smiling at me as I sat at the table for snack time. I must have been hungrier than usual; I had two more slices.

Chapter 3

There had been no funeral. Grandmommy's ashes arrived in a small box labeled "Cremains"; I wondered what happened to that box. Mom never told me. Mom had moved on, accepting the death faster and better than I did. Although I still wished she would come talk to me about Grandmommy and the circumstances of her death, I long ago gave up hope that she would open my bedroom door for a heart-to-heart talk with me. Heart-to-hearts were just not her style.

Mom didn't say much about Grandmommy. Each day, she and I went through the day, speaking of logistics, sharing the basic, day-to-day operations: the time and place of school activities, pickups, drop-offs, meals, and classroom necessities. We didn't talk about Grandmommy. We didn't talk about her, although my heart yearned to know more about her. My aching heart felt incomplete. Without a funeral, without talking about her, my heart had no closure. A loud silent gap remained between me and Mom.

"Grandmommy died of pancreatic cancer," Mom finally said. "It was sudden, and there was nothing we could have done. There is nothing the doctors could do. You'll be starting a new school in the fall. Let's focus on that. Be brave and strong. We will be okay."

I didn't press her for more details. I knew not to ask; she wouldn't answer my questions. I knew she loved me. I knew she would do everything she could to keep us safe, to keep us together. This was really all I needed to know. It was just me and Mom now, just the two of us. It was probably better if I just stayed quietly in the background, letting her handle life for us both.

I wished I had a sibling, someone to share this experience with, someone to help me understand the pain I felt. I wished I had close family I could call. Cousins from my dad's family lived nearby, but I didn't feel close to them. Not close enough to call for help. So many confusing feelings and conflicting questions went through my mind. Death felt heavy. Maybe that's why we didn't talk. Death was dark, depressing, and sad. No one wanted to talk about this kind of stuff, especially with me; I was just a kid. It was best if I kept my feelings to myself. No one wanted me to remind them of death and loss. I guessed I shouldn't talk about it.

I was abruptly awakened by the pilot's announcement: "We are beginning our descent into Dusseldorf. We will be landing soon." The familiar nauseating feeling returned. I hoped the family was there. I hoped Ingrid would be with them; she was the only person I knew there. I had not seen her in over a year, since Grandmommy's death.

Chapter 4

The mother of the house in Germany was intimidating. She was part of Mom's past, although I didn't exactly know how. Mom spent four years in Germany before immigrating to the United States. She didn't share; I didn't ask. Mrs. Schmidt seemed okay, if one followed the rules (rules I had yet to be made aware of). I was confident I would be made aware of them in time. The house felt strict, more intense than I was used to. Even though it was summer, the sky was gray, and the buildings were damp and cold, accurately mirroring my emotions. Mrs. Schmidt sits beside me with her two daughters, aware of my malaise. Together at dinner, the first leg of my summer plans were discussed. I would be in Germany a few days, and then we would all be traveling to their summer home in Italy. Seven to ten days later, my aunt was to meet us and take me to Montpellier, France. I would spend the remaining weeks with family in France. It all felt methodically organized and to the point. Feeling oddly reassured, I fell asleep. There was a plan, and I was made aware of the plans in advance.

The vibrant colors of Italy lifted my spirit. The sun offered daily kisses on my skin. The ocean air whispered healing notes in my ear. Feeling free to explore the neighborhood alone, the vibrant summer colors along the walkways left a trail for me to find my way back. Every store became more alive than the last, the local summer produce and market goods on full display. I visited my favorite local delicatessen every day, my French mannerisms assimilating quickly to warm bread and cheese for a midmorning snack. Returning each afternoon, I quickly adopted the Italian way of a midafternoon gelato. With my American-accented French and deliberate attempts to incorporate the few Italian words I was learning, the store owners smiled and welcomed me back each day to teach me my word of the day, usually corresponding to the gelato flavor of the day. My secret pleasure was making sure to order a different flavor each visit, just to try them all.

Alone, enjoying my snacks, I felt free. There was no one I needed to engage with, no one I needed to try to understand, no unstated rules I needed to interpret. I didn't need to read anyone's mind to know what I was supposed to do. I could just sit with my bread, cheese, and gelato; no need to explain to anyone, no need to ask permission. No need to disguise my feelings. No need to feel anything. Maybe this trip would turn out okay after all, even better than I thought.

It was too early for dinner with the family, but I was hungry. I sized up the contents in the refrigerator; a lonely piece of cheese begged me to eat it, so I did: a nice snack to hold me over. An unspoken rule made its presence known. With her curled lips and wrinkled nose, Mrs. Schmidt made her disgust over my action quite clear. Embarrassed to be caught eating unauthorized food, the lemon gelato and cheese made its way to my throat in a liquid vurp (vomit burp). How could I be so stupid? I should have known better; this was not my house. I could not just help myself to whatever I wanted.

Two days later, Mrs. Schmidt informed me the plans had changed. My aunt was no longer coming to pick me up. I would be sent by train to Montpellier. Again, I was being sent away. I guess Mrs. Schmidt changed her mind about having me with her family. I must be too much trouble to put up with.

I boarded the train with twelve sandwiches (six Nutella and six cheese). I promised myself to only eat one per hour, ensuring enough for the ten-hour ride.

I pretended to read, but my attentive eyes were on each passenger's gestures. It was a full cabin, exchanging people at stops every hour. I wondered if people noticed I was traveling alone. I wondered if they even saw me. I removed the plastic "Minor Traveling Alone" announcement from my neck, hoping to inconspicuously blend in. Wanting to go unnoticed, I made no sound. I closed my eyes, pretending to sleep, but the sound of a rustling newspaper became louder. The smell of cigarette smoke filled the cabin. The thought of chocolate Nutella called to me. I was hungry.

It was okay, rationing my one sandwich. Still hungry, I helped myself to a second, vowing this would be all I ate for now. My hunger was augmented by the sounds and smells of so many strangers. I devoured all twelve sandwiches before the halfway mark. What was I going to do next? Although I was full, what if I got hungry again? What an undisciplined child I was.

Chapter 5

My *tante* greeted me in Montpellier; it was finally my turn to get off the train, escaping the stench of cigarette smoke. Finally, I could inhale fully. My tante's warm embrace soothed my frazzled nerves. The last time I was in her home, I was with my mom and Grandmommy. There was no mention of Grandmommy as I entered; they never did get along. Every visit I could remember ended with an argument. My six cousins had since moved out, offering me a choice of whichever room I wanted. I chose Isabelle's room. Being the closest to my age and having spent the most time with her, I felt the most connection to her.

Mom called. Hearing her voice on the phone made the lump in my throat swell. It had been only six days since I last hugged her. I missed her so much. She shared with me her projects of wallpapering her room and painting mine; I sensed her time without me was good for her. I wished I was home to paint with her, just to be in the room with her, even if we didn't speak; I was painfully aware of the distance between us.

Tomorrow, Isabelle and Eric were coming to see me. My aching heart would feel better in the morning to see them. In the meantime, my lonely heart cried to sleep.

A commotion in the kitchen awakened me. Isabelle was here! I rushed into the kitchen and hugged her. Feeling Grandmommy's spirit flowing between us, I couldn't let go. She sat at the table and cried with me. This was the first time I cried for Grandmommy's death; Isabelle understood.

"Ma petite cousine," she said, although I was taller than her now; her tears comfort me.

Finally, I felt safe. I was okay there. My afflicted heart was consoled by the mixture of hugs, tears, and buttered *tartines.* Even the normally odd-tasting, unrefrigerated French milk-in-a-box cocoa tasted great that morning.

I loved my cousin Isabelle. I've known her husband, Eric, since I was five or six. Together, they owned a floral business, growing and selling flowers at the farmers markets. I was delighted to share my days with them; it soothed my raw, tender heart. Taking me in, incorporating me into their lives, I felt wanted.

I helped out at their shop; they showed me how to measure the necessary seedling depth. I appreciated the solitude with my fingers in the dirt, watching Eric and Isabelle repotting and labeling flowers and plants, making preparations for tomorrow's market. Eagerly contributing as I could, I daydreamed about what would happen at the market tomorrow. Content to spend the days with them, my connection with them offered a sense of solid ground that had eluded me this entire trip.

At four in the morning, wet drips of drool replaced any need of an alarm clock. It was Vidock, the family Leonberger. His enormous head stood eye level to me while I lay in the bed. I squished my nose at the stench of his heavy breathing, and drips of drool landed on my face. I secretly loved the morning wakeup call from this spectacular, unfamiliar breed, a cartoon version of a great Dane, Bernese mountain dog, Newfoundland, and Saint Bernard combined. I was ready for whatever today's market had planned for me; the lightness of the spring in my step announced to me I was in the right place. I was going to be okay.

We unloaded the truck; the floral array displayed their allure to the public, their scent gripping the noses of even the most hardened faces. Summer's fullest expression of life, the vibrant colors were in full bloom. When we took a breakfast break, Eric introduced me to the local baker, trying to engage me in conversation. The melting chocolate leaking through the croissant seams hijacked my attention. Charmed by my American-accented French, the baker offered me a second one. Reveling, I accepted.

Speaking French fluently, I took on the task of wrapping each patron's chosen bouquet, giving me the chance to learn more, engaging with joyful people while helping my cousins. Feeling both useful and appreciated, I continued to feel my heart mending. My summer days were filled with my loving cousins, joyful exchanges with local patrons, cheese and meat delicacies at the market, two (sometimes three) *pains au chocolat*; my broken heart was on the mend.

Chapter 6

"We will be landing in San Francisco, where the temperature is a cool 64 degrees and skies are clear; attendants, prepare for landing."

Almost home. I knew Mom was waiting for me; she told me she would be at the gate. I knew she would be there. I wanted so badly to be home. I missed her so much. I missed being home. It had been almost twelve weeks. I hoped she never sent me away again.

Walking on tiptoes through the tunnel, I saw her. I caught her eye as I jumped up and peered above the sea of people embracing their loved ones. That would be me and my mom soon; her eyes on me, I felt her anticipating my arrival. I ran the final ten yards, unable to contain my tears; they rolled down my cheeks with joy. Tears steadily flowing, she engulfed me in her arms, squeezing me as tight as her five-foot frame could muster. I was unwilling to pull away; hugs like this were rare. Consoled by Mom's hugs, tears, and delightful squeals of joy to see me, I was completely open and vulnerable to receive all of her love and affection. I knew Mom loved me. She really loved me. She really missed me.

Exposed, I was unprepared for the scornful look of disgust that appeared on her brow.

"These are not your clothes," she snapped. "Where are your clothes?"

"None of my clothes fit," I explained, "so Isabelle gave me hers."

Silently acknowledging my undeniably large weight gain, Mom looked with contempt as she absorbed the scope of my body's changes in her absence. Her downturned mouth and clenched jaw opted to mute whatever unkind words were at the tip of her tongue. Once again, her silence stabbed my heart, letting all of the love bleed out.

Back at the house, the fresh paint of my new lavender walls offered no consolation.

Eighth grade orientation was the following week. My dignity drained with each attempt to find uniform clothes in the store that would fit my size 14/16 frame. I was crying on the hideous crumpled pile of uniforms on my bed when Mom summoned me to run errands.

"What's wrong with you?" she blurted out.

With more force and intensity than the question warranted, I unleashed my fury.

"I hate you," I cried. "I wish I had a different mother. If you are too stupid to know what's wrong, then you don't deserve to know." I followed this up with the unedited vulgarities my cousins took delight in making sure I pronounced correctly. I hurled every French obscenity I knew, in a manner no child should ever speak to any adult, especially not to one's mother.

I wanted to hurt my mom; without hitting her, this was the best idea I could come up with. I wanted to cause her emotional harm, trying to inflict the same emotional pain I was feeling yet unable to express.

"Just who the hell do you think you are?" Mom snapped. "I don't know what happened to you. I don't know who you are. Call your father. Tell him to pick you up. You can go live with him. You're not welcome in my house, speaking to me like you just did. You have from now until dinner to decide."

I had gone too far; I wished I could retract the hatred I unleashed on her. Desperate to return to normalcy, I tried to apologize, but she was unwilling to accept; we continued the week in silence until school started. Something had changed. I felt it; I knew it. Although I could not say with certainty or clarity exactly what it was, something was now different between us. My mistake was too big to forgive, too harsh to be undone. I supposed Mom still loved me. I now knew she just didn't like me.

Chapter 7

The thirty additional pounds I gained made me feel more isolated and separate from my eighth grade classmates than I did as the new kid in school only a year earlier.

We all wore the same uniform; however, mine was the only one that flared out at the hips from the additional material of my larger size. The amount of blue plaid material needed to cover my butt and reach the required knee length made me feel exceedingly large and unsightly. I was humiliated and kept my head down; averting any eye contact seemed my only protection. My head and my heart pulled in opposite directions when I heard Suzie screeching my name down the hall. I was torn between wanting to shriek my finest eighth grade girl squeal in response and wanting Suzie to shut up, to stop any unsolicited undesirable attention.

Suzie became my best friend the very first day of seventh grade. There was nowhere for me to hide as the new student. I appreciated the school uniform as my shield then; a navy-blue skirt and white shirt rendered me invisible (or at least neutral).

I was relieved to be in a small private school, but as I took my seat in the first period class, religion, panic rose. Even the uniform could not hide my emerging embarrassment as the class began its morning religious rituals. I didn't know any of the prayers or accompanying hand gestures. With growing discomfort heating my skin, I didn't know the basic chapters in the Bible everyone was turning to. Mom and I didn't have any form of religion or ceremony in our home. God was absent where we lived.

"Don't worry. I don't know the words either, and I've been in this school since first grade," said a girl with the sweetest smile. "I'm Suzie."

Grateful for a friendly welcome, I could feel the heat on my face dissipate. "Hi," I replied. "Can you help me find the right place in the Bible?"

"Girls, do I need to separate you two on the first day of school?" our teacher said.

Giggling and hiding from the teacher's view, I instantly knew I was going to be okay, as Suzie's goofy expression mimicking the teacher made me laugh. Welcoming Suzie's lifeline of friendship, I accepted. I needed a friend.

Suzie and I had grown close in our first year. Today, after the entire summer apart, I feel so distant.

Trying to read Suzie's mind, too afraid to hear her words about my frumpy appearance, I made an excuse about being needed in the office. I quickly hugged her and promised to catch up with her later. I bolted into the bathrooms to hide. Suzie was the most popular girl in school. Uncertain about how my weight gain would affect our friendship, I opted to avoid the uncomfortable possibility of a school year without her.

Sitting in homeroom, Suzie was a few rows over; she waved at me. The palpitations in my heart subsided, realizing my friendship with Suzie was secure. I returned the wave and relaxed in my chair. Making her way to me after the bell, Suzie reminded me of rapidly approaching cheerleading tryouts. Although we were on the squad the previous year, we still needed to try out; there were no guarantees or special treatment. We all met at lunch for the details.

All the girls, returning cheer squad team and hopefuls, congregated poolside prior to the meeting. Their perfectly pressed, pleated skirts showed off the newest curves and puberty growth developments from the summer. I was the only one who still looked like a child, wearing no makeup, two braids in my hair, and a bra that was not yet necessary, except for the fat accumulation where breasts would be, had they developed. They shared their summer experiences, going on vacation with their families to the beach, mountains, rivers, and lakes; I was not interested in sharing my events. Without embellishing, I gave my itinerary account of my summer, garnering some favor in the prospect of my European travels alone. Purposely omitting most of the events of my trip, the version I shared sounded more alive and exciting than the one I actually experienced. I envied their accounts of time with their families, including siblings, grandparents, cousins, and other relatives that all seemed blissfully all coexisting and laughing and generally enjoying each other's company.

My relief turned to disbelief. The cheerleading skirts revealed my excess weight. Fuck no, I didn't want to try out. Nonetheless, I stayed throughout the meeting. My focus turned to the distance between my mom, as it seemed to grow more insurmountable with each day of silence that passed between us. I really was an ass. I really damaged our relationship. No girl here would ever talk to her mother the way I had. Better they not know what a shitty person I was. What other girl here would be so despicable that their own mother wanted to send them away and get rid of them? No one, I suspected, only me.

Chapter 8

It was the second week of eighth grade. Now the number of days we participated in PE counted toward our grade.

Fuck, what a humiliating part of eighth grade. We all changed in the open room. There was no hiding who added "good weight" in just the right places on their body. This was not me. I was part of the group that just got fat.

Hanging my navy blue skirt on the hook, my mother's disgust hovering over me in the room, my humiliation soared as I feared the forty-six eyes criticizing my body from behind.

I had a round face, pudgy belly, and thighs so swollen that they rubbed together in our required red "dolphin shorts." Walking laps, my thighs rubbed together and began to sweat; a red rash began to form. Whatever popularity currency I earned from my trip to Europe diminished with each lap around the blacktop, as big sweat stains began to form in the armpits of my fire engine red PE shirt. There was nowhere for me to hide. Not only had I grown out during the summer, I grew up. Standing at five feet, seven inches tall, a full three inches taller than most of my classmates, I tried to conceal myself, which proved useless.

I dreading the school year; week two had just begun. It was the second day of full-dress PE. I didn't wash my PE clothes from the day before, and the previous day's stains were highly noticeable. Fuck. Eighth grade was just getting worse each day. Today's PE lesson: volleyball. I had played on the school team in seventh grade. Although I still needed to learn all of the rules, I felt myself stand straight as we made our way onto the courts.

Four of last year's teammates were chosen to choose four teams. Lining up on the back line, sweat droplets made their way down my vertebrae as names were about to be called. I heard my name. What? I was called first; picked first? Really? Exhaling relief, I high-five my captain as I lined up behind her. I hoped that with my weight, I can still jump high. I hoped I could still spike the ball over the net or block. I hope my team wasn't expecting me to play as I did last year; I weighed too much now. I hoped my added height would make up the difference.

With the first hit across the net, the sensations of playing perked up every cell in my body. With the process of reacquainting my body with the game, I felt the surge of life flowing below the weight I carried; the physical weight melted away as the emotional weight of humiliation also disappeared.

Oh wow, I missed volleyball. I didn't know how much I loved playing, until then. With the team wins accumulating, laughter, more high-fives, and team cheers erupted. Right now, my peers and I were equal. I felt accepted.

When PE ended, we rushed to the showers. The chatter about who was kissing who, who had a crush on who, and the upcoming cheerleading tryouts hummed in the background. While I could hear it, I felt no desire to engage. I savored the feelings of today. I needed to feel more of what I was feeling, the euphoria of playing volleyball. This year, there would be tryouts for the girls' volleyball team; in seventh grade, the team accepted everyone who wanted to play. I couldn't wait.

Last year, I played as an activity, just something to do while waiting for my mom to pick me up after school. This year was different. I wanted to play and play well. I wanted to try out. I had not felt excited about participating in anything since I quit ice skating when we moved.

Changing into school uniform, I forgot about my weight. I forgot about cheerleading tryouts. I forgot about my mom. I forgot about my grandmother. For a moment, I felt happy. I forgot about everything that was my life.

Chapter 9

We sat on the bleachers; my feet bounced on the metal bleachers, the rhythmic pounding on the metal focusing my attention. Just one year earlier, I was the new girl in school. Many of these girls had welcomed me. Now, feeling like competitors, we all sat in the discomfort, wondering, waiting on the coach to tell us who would be chosen for this year's volleyball team.

"Natacha Nelson."

My name; I heard my name. This was the same feeling I had atop the ice skating podium when I was eight years old.

My stomach vibrated; uncertain if my voice would betray me, I opted to not speak, just letting my larger-than-expected toothy grin acknowledge my accomplishment. I gazed down, distracted by the dried gum on the bleacher; I listened as other names were announced. These girls had known each other since elementary school. Although a year had passed, I was still the new girl. I still felt like an outsider.

At the first formal team practice, my position was clearly marked. As a front row outside hitter, my job was to hit the ball over the net as hard as I possibly could, while stretching my hands out to block any opposing player from doing the same. At five feet eight inches tall, I was capable of doing my job well. I love playing volleyball. The feeling of competing with teammates was new. My years of ice skating competition were solo.

On the court, a healing energy oozed through my cells, opening an electric surge that both soothed and energized me. Joy grew as I connected with my team, as we played our hearts out and competed for one another.

Mom was indifferent about my playing on the team. She was relieved I had a safe place to be while I waited for her after school. Although she attended and cheered for us at many of our home games, she never seemed to smile the same way as she did while I was ice skating. Her beaming smiles of joy eluded me on the volleyball court. Her lackluster presence was not lost on me.

Ice skating felt like a distant part of my past, although it had only been a year since I last laced my skates, hearing the crunching sound of newly sharpened blades slice the ice. Skating had been my companion from age seven through eleven.

The skating rink offered solace for me. It was a place that felt safe. For countless hours, I could get lost in creating choreography, incorporating higher jumps, and practicing new spins. My hours on the ice, I felt I was doing exactly what I was supposed to be doing, feeling no need to do anything or be anything else. I could get lost, disconnecting my mind from my home.

I missed skating. I missed Mom's excitement when I added a new skating element into my repertoire, moving up the rankings. I miss her delight in stopping for fresh donuts after early Sunday morning practices.

I loved volleyball, but it lacked the element of shared joy Mom and I engaged in together. Those days with my mom were gone; I left them in San Jose when we moved last year.

Our new home was too far from the old skating rink; the commute was no longer feasible. We scouted the local rink with intentions of continuing. I tried different coaches but did not connect with any of them. I no longer felt free during free skate time. The other skaters and their parents stared, questioning who was I to intrude on their space. There were rules I was not privy to. They made comments about my unorthodox athletic style and said

I was too big to be a real skater. I was not welcome, the energy from the members informed me. No words were necessary; I could feel it. Not sure what it was, but I knew I would never skate again.

On my final day skating, Mom drove home from the rink; my silence was loud. My love of skating was extinguished, yet I could not put into words what I was feeling. I could not share with Mom what happened. I felt unsure of what happened. I sat in the car and said nothing.

"We need to leave in an hour to go to the rink," Mom said the following Saturday morning.

"I am not going," I replied. "I am never skating again."

"What do you mean, you don't want to skate anymore? You are just going to quit? I worked overtime to buy those skates; they cost over five hundred dollars! You've had them for less than a month, not even breaking them in, and now you want to quit?"

"Give them away to some other little girl who wants them," I snapped. "I'm never going back there."

I fell on my bed and cried. I loved my new skates. They were custom-made S.P. Terry's, made just for my feet, the kind all real professional competitors wore. Mom had worked so hard to buy me those skates, and I knew it.

Mom's disgust at me weighed heavy in my heart. I knew how hard she worked to save the money for these skates that now sat unused in their red bag. What a disappointment I must have been to her. Such an ungrateful daughter, to behave with such disregard for her efforts to provide for me. I didn't deserve her. I betrayed her with my selfishness. I hurt her with my childish behavior. Not even the growing shame was enough to bring me back to the skating rink. I just could not ever bring myself to go back there.

As the volleyball season came to an end, a pain in my heart began to surface: the fear of not having a team to be with, to fit in with, to participate in one common goal with. Just as the fears continued to rise, a possibility appeared: basketball team tryouts.

Making the basketball team was comforting, as many of the volleyball girls also played basketball. I was comforted by my new role as a r ebounder. Basketball provided me with an outlet to focus on, yet I did not hold the same reverence for that game as I did for volleyball. I loved my team, the camaraderie, and the competition. Basketball offered me a distraction from the day-to-day undercurrent of sadness that still lingered with me. I loved that basketball was a place to hide, a distraction, a place to not feel what I was really feeling.

While volleyball brought me joy and peace, basketball kept me from feeling anything. Ironically, I would later gain accolades for my basketball skills, not volleyball.

Chapter 10

The eighth grade curriculum in a private school pushed my academic abilities past my comfort level. It wasn't impossible, but much more effort was required. Taking exams at this level was a new skill I had to learn. The depth of concepts and detail of material was more intense than I had been exposed to.

The use of words like *dumb* and *stupid* was forbidden in our home. Mom was physically revolted by the sound of these words. While I never felt dumb or stupid in school, I didn't feel smart, either. *Smart* was not the word choice to describe me. Academics required more work for me than seemed necessary for others. I needed twice as long to complete reading assignments as my classmates. Math concepts needed to marinate in my mind before the aha moment would hit me. I like school. I liked learning. I just didn't like that I needed longer than most to learn.

Not like Elizabeth, one of my best childhood friends. Elizabeth was considered smart. She loved to study and was a disciplined student, willing to study in all of her free hours. I admired her dedication to studying; in elementary school, she committed to waking up in the early hours before school to study. She was always willing to read more and do more to be ahead. She would skip television for additional time to read.

While I felt content to be a decent student, Elizabeth thrived at being an exceptional one. I admired her quality that I lacked. I, however, was not the only one who noticed.

Mom always sang praises to Elizabeth's work ethic and for her willingness to forgo playing for reading.

"Elizabeth is so good," she'd say. "Elizabeth is so smart. Elizabeth works so hard. Elizabeth takes school so seriously; she never needs her mom to ask if her work is done. I am glad you are friends; maybe some of that will rub off on you."

With every tuition payment and report card received from my new school, Mom would repeat the same tune in my head. I was well aware of Mom working two jobs for me to receive a private school education; the heavy weight on my shoulders was wearisome.

Mom never actually asked about test scores or grades; she didn't need to.

"I wish I could be more like Elizabeth," I'd say. "I don't know why I don't want to work as hard as she does. I think there's something wrong with the way my brain works; it just doesn't work the same way as hers. Getting honor roll and straight As just isn't for me."

In elementary school, I was fine. But now, grades mattered. They meant so much more now. I needed to figure this school thing out or risk being left behind. The faint voice in my head began to speak more boldly, more convincingly. My old ways of being were outdated; a new way of being needed to emerge.

Every moment after school, while waiting for practice, after dinner, and early hours before class was now filled with schoolwork. I stayed up as long as necessary to complete all required assignments, making sure to read the accompanying references and footnotes.

Within weeks, there was a noticeable difference. The depths of detail I would recount for tests astonished me. There was a surge of pride as details from random readings would come to me in class; I was able to answer questions posed by the teachers, using many details the other students had missed.

I had a new sense of confidence in my brain's ability as I made my way through classes. As my grades steadily began to rise, so did my belief that maybe I could be smart too. Teachers were not the only ones to notice. Mom was aware of my additional study hours and rewarded me by bringing additional snacks to my room. Along with the snacks, she offered smiles of delight in the new me. Her pleasure even extended through kisses on my cheek.

One night's reading assignment was to complete twenty pages in our book; I exceeded that by finishing the whole thing. I was high on Mom's approval of the new me. The fatigue I felt the next day was exceeded by the satisfaction of a perfect score on our pop quiz, including bonus points reading ahead.

"Ha, I was prepared for you," I told my teacher with a smirk. I felt like I had outsmarted her. I felt smart. I woke up a part of myself I did not know existed. The smart girl in me was beginning to show up, and I liked her.

That day, I created a new rule for myself: "Do as much as possible to stay ahead. Be more prepared than asked, more than is expected. Do more than the coaches expect. But don't let anyone see how hard you're working. Be like a duck: smooth on the surface but paddling like mad underwater. Don't show how much effort it takes. Showing effort can be seen as a sign of weakness. Don't let anyone find out how much energy you're exerting; don't acknowledge how hard it feels."

My plan worked. No one ever knew I was a slow reader. No one seemed to care about the excess weight I carried. No one knew my mom worked two jobs and we barely survived. No own noticed I didn't have a father. No one ever learned how poor we were. Putting forth academic and athletic successes seemed to render our faults invisible.

For the first time, I could say, "I feel smart. I feel witty. I feel powerful, and I feel in control."

Chapter 11

Entering high school, I felt different. Although junior high and high school classes shared the same building, our uniform colors separated us. Moving up meant trading in my navy blue for what felt like an upgrade: a choice of green, yellow, khaki, or gray pants or skirt to be worn with our white shirt.

With the softer boundaries of our new uniform came the flexibility of our schedules; we were given the option to choose our classes and schedule. For me, this meant conferencing with Suzie to pair up as many of our classes as possible.

For Algebra II, I chose the same teacher I had for Algebra I. He was the kind of math teacher I wished all kids could have; it was an honor learning from him. He was tough but fair; showing your work was valued, not just the final answers. I negotiated every portion of a point for math problems where my final answer was incorrect but where I could show my processing was on point. I haggled every point as if my grade depended on my verbal skills as much as my math skills, because for me to pass, it did.

Math was the only course I could not go ahead of the class. I could not read ahead and do the work in advance to stay a few steps ahead of the teacher's lesson plan, leaving me uncomfortable and vulnerable when I could not keep up.

I had the same seat in every other class: first row, far right. I sat slightly sideways, leaning on the wall, legs stretched, leaning on the desk arm to write. I was close enough to pay attention but inconspicuous enough when I wanted to be left out.

In math, though, I chose the back row. I needed to keep a low profile; I kept my head down and did not draw any attention to myself. I didn't want to be called on to solve a problem on the chalkboard in front of the class.

Believing my first week of ninth grade math was successfully completed, I was startled when the teacher asked to see me after school.

"You are a hard-working student," he began, "and it shows. I know you'll be able to pass this course. Last year, while you passed, you were always teetering on the edge. I had hoped you would have taken the recommended summer math to strengthen your skills. You should pass this year; however, it may be a constant struggle for you to stay at the level of your classmates."

Time really seemed to slow to a crawl as he said what I most feared:

"I think you should consider repeating eighth grade Algebra I to fully grasp all of the concepts and create a stronger foundation in math. Your ability to take higher math, chemistry, and physics classes will depend on your proficiency now. Of course, it's your choice; you don't have to repeat it. Take the weekend to think about your decision and let me know Monday."

There is was: proof that I was not as smart as I tried to be. I was sick to my stomach now that the truth was revealed; by Monday, the entire school would know what I knew now. I decided to repeat the class.

Humiliated, I sat in eighth grade math class, unable to conceal my khaki skirt among the sea of navy blue. All that was left for me to do was smile as big as possible to camouflage the shame that hijacked my body.

Chapter 12

It turned out there was a benefit to repeating a class. I knew what was coming in advance and was able to divert time away from math to get ahead in other classes. At the end of freshman year, my grades were stellar, and I played both volleyball and basketball. A buzz was emanating from me; a top-performing student-athlete was beginning to emerge, solidifying my prominent place in high school, a place I made sure no one would doubt. I knew I earned my accomplishments; I just needed to make sure no one found out my secret. If anyone were to find out my secret, I would make my mom transfer me to another school, the humiliation would be too damaging to overcome.

I went to the principal's office after finishing my final exams to schedule my summer work hours. Mom and I had made an agreement with the school that I would work as a custodian during the summer to pay a portion of my tuition. Degraded, I begin my work: scraping gum off all the desks and chairs, scrubbing all the lockers with bleach, and giving each classroom a fresh coat of paint.

I was jealous of other students who were free to take summer classes to skip ahead for the upcoming school year. Disgust and resentment toward my mom intensified. I cowered in the locked classrooms while I worked, making sure no one ever saw me.

Each day, my resentment turned to anger. By summer's end, my anger festered into rage. The silence was loud in our home. There was nothing I could say to Mom. Actually, there was plenty I wished to say, but I knew not to speak. I didn't look at her. I didn't want to eat dinner in the same room with her. I shut my mouth, fearing one word would earn me a one-way ticket to my father's house.

One day, feeling the acid of hatred fill my stomach, I opted to eat ice cream for dinner, hoping the cold, sweet treat would soothe the vile taste intruding my taste buds. There was a rage inside of me. I felt it wanting to be let out, but I couldn't. The rage oozed from me; I needed to contain it before I caused irreparable damage. I found music to blunt the edge. The lyrics of Depeche Mode aligned with my mood. Ice cream subdued the hot rage burning in me. Once calm, my uneaten dinner appealed to me. After finishing, I had some toasted bread slathered with Nutella and felt calm enough to go to bed.

I was frightened by the intensity of my rage. I feared it would seep out and betray me. I was afraid I would betray myself and make known the cause of my rage. I was constantly afraid my peers would find out I was a fraud, that I didn't belong in this prestigious private school. I was constantly afraid someone would see me and discover my secret, that Mom and I were poor, that we couldn't afford the same luxurious lifestyle they enjoyed.

I knew that if my secret came to light, or if my rage was to escape, I would be caught. I no longer would be the happy, fun girl everyone thought I was. If my rage was unleashed, I wouldn't be able to control what I said or did. I inherited my father's gift of rage; I was just like him.

I needed to squelch my rage. I needed to control it, suppress it, no matter what. This was rule number one, above all others that Mom expected from me, and I now expected from myself.

Mom's first rule was to never let anyone ever see what you're feeling inside, especially anger, because other people can use your anger against you. Any form of anger meant you were out of control and vulnerable; you were weak if you were angry. Someone could see your vulnerability and use it to harm you. You must stay in control at all times.

Staying in control at all times was important to me, even more crucial than being calm like a duck. I had to stay in control of my life, at all costs.

The rage was burning inside of me and gaining intensity with each day.

"You are just like your father," Mom told me.

This rage in me was the same rage that was in him. I was my father's daughter. I was just like him. And I hated him.

Chapter 13

Once school resumed, I was happy to get back to the normal rhythm of classes. I could let my guard down slightly; the threat of being caught as the school's janitor ceased. I exhaled a little easier as sophomore year continued. I maintained my grades while playing two sports. There was relief in the predictability of my routines.

One day, when I climbed into the car after practice, Mom announced, "It's time."

"Time for what?" I asked.

"Time for you to get a job," she replied.

A job? I thought. *I don't have time for a job.*

Didn't she see that my schedule was full with sports and schoolwork? I didn't have a car, not even a license to drive. She couldn't do this to me. Why did I need to get a job?

"There is a Sizzler restaurant down the street," she continued. "I will take you. You'll need to go in, ask for the manager, and apply for whatever position they have available."

My rage monster was awakened. I could feel its energy coursing through my body. *Just smile*, I told myself. That afternoon, we drove to the restaurant, and I went inside.

"We have a hostess position available," the manager said. "What kind of hours are you looking for?"

"Mostly weekends," I replied, "and some weekday evenings, depending on my sports schedule and classes." I secretly hoped my lack of flexibility would dissuade him from hiring me.

"You can start this Friday at four o'clock. The pay is $3.25 per hour."

$3.25 per hour? I thought, pleased. That was a dollar more than I was earning at school. If I worked enough hours here, maybe I could get out of working at the school next summer. I agreed and started that week.

The Friday night shift was lively. The energy of the waitstaff, cooks, and bar hosts was welcoming. My smile throughout the evening was genuine, I actually enjoyed working at the restaurant with this group. I loved earning money doing work that was fun. As a bonus, I was out of the house Friday evenings, away from Mom's critical eye. Secretly, I was happy she made me get this job. But I wasn't going to give her the satisfaction of knowing it.

Within the month, I was promoted to waiting tables, which meant I collected tips. Tips earned were my business; no one needed to know how much I earned. My bright smile, fast pace, and customer service earned me cash in my pocket. I gave my paychecks to Mom, but the cash on hand was mine to use in whatever manner I chose.

I now had a taste of freedom. I worked additional hours when I could and saved most of my tip money. I started junior year of high school without missing a beat. Suzie and I were still best friends, and I juggled sports, classes, and work. I felt confident and in control of my life, the world I created for myself. My rage monster seemed to go away.

My relationship with Mom was no longer as edgy. Our relationship was now that we coexisted. We talked about our day and shared the functional, practical needs of our day-to-day lives. She attended most of our home games, which surprised me. For many games, she was the only parent there to cheer for us. I really liked having her there, feeling her support all of us. She was a mother figure for all my teammates.

With junior year in full swing, I was reminded every day of the need for my record to remain impeccable, from grades to sports to after-school activities. This was the year to apply for college admissions. This was the year that mattered most if I wanted to continue my education in a private university. With my eyes set on college, I increased the intensity of school and focused on the possibility of a sports scholarship.

I thought, *There was no way I could work enough at the restaurant to pay for college, and there was no way Mom could afford tuition at Santa Clara University. I had to get a scholarship; it was my only option.*

In the meantime, the boys in my school seemed to have developed their cuteness factor overnight. Maybe I had been too busy to notice. Well, now I noticed, although the prospect of dating made my stomach flutter. I was too nervous to consider more than friendship. Anxiety flushed through me whenever I visualized myself dating a guy. I was intimidated by the fact that some girls already had sex. I kept my growing feelings for one boy secret, even from Suzie. As long as I maintained my friendship with all the guys, no one would notice I liked one in a different way. I especially could not let *him* know.

Chapter 14

Working at Sizzler enabled me to keep my grades at the level I demanded from myself, as well as save money for a new car. I diligently saved money for two years, and as the school break approached, my excitement grew as my additional work hours would put me well in range.

For the past year, Mom and I had been able to be together without any feelings of animosity between us.

One day, however, Mom came to me and said, "We need to talk." Her quivering yet stern voice jolted my heart rate up.

"What's up, Mom?" I asked casually, smiling.

"How much money do you have saved?" she asked.

"Almost three thousand," I said. "Why?"

"I need to borrow it to pay rent for the next few months," Mom said softly. "Sales at work haven't been good. My commissions aren't coming in. I may not have a job next month. Make sure not to spend too much through the holidays. And see if you can work additional hours while you are off from school."

At that moment, I really loathed my mom. I silently screamed with all my might, *Fuck! Fuck you, Mom!* Every cell in my body wailed in unison. I summoned every ounce of inner discipline I could muster to contain my rage, which was on the edge of erupting violently.

I clenched my teeth, smiled, and said, "I understand. I will get it for you."

But I didn't understand. I couldn't understand why we were in this situation again.

"I promise I'll pay you back," she said. "This is just a loan. Keep track of how much I owe you."

"Okay," I replied. "I will," thinking, *I'll add it to the previous monies borrowed, in hopes of one day being paid back.*

It was not okay. This was not all right at all. Borrowing my money to pay rent was not okay. Using my money for us to live was not okay. I was not okay with any of this. I was not supposed to work for tuition and now rent. What the fuck was she doing with her money?

Why is money so difficult for you to figure out, Mom? I thought bitterly. *Why has money plagued you as long as I can remember?* We lived in four different apartments in the last five years, each one smaller than the last.

The hardship and despair Mom carried was palpable. What an asshole daughter I was for my critical, insensitive judgments of her. As long as I kept them to myself, it was okay. No need to let on that I could see her anguish. No need to highlight her feelings of dejection, weighing her with any guilt or shame for the financial mess we were in.

Many days, I packed my lunch with whatever food donations my mom received from church. I rarely invited friends to our home, fearing our one-bedroom apartment would reveal our ugly secret of poverty.

I took my savings jar, put on a brave face, and gave her the entire jar, avoiding eye contact to ensure my feelings of betrayal were not recognized. Mom needed to see my resolute face, the one that let her know I was okay, I was strong, we would survive. The valiant daughter was the one mom liked most.

Five years earlier was my first experience. Elizabeth's mother, Mom's friend, made out bed on the floor as comfortable as she knew how. She padded the floor with every blanket she could find and gave us clean sheets to lie on.

"We will only need to stay here for a few weeks at most," Mom said then.

But a few weeks became two months. Two months that Mom and I slept on the floor of Elizabeth's room, having been forced out of our home next door. Without the money for security deposit and first and last month's rent, we were unable to move to our own apartment. We settled for a safe place to sleep, to shower and dress ourselves to be presentable to the world.

That was how seventh grade began. No one knew that we were homeless for this period of time. I could hear Mom crying herself to sleep as she held my hand under the blankets. I kept my back turned to her, allowing her the dignity to not let on I could hear her.

I didn't know how we ended up homeless, sleeping on the floor of our neighbor's bedroom. Life was changing too fast for me to make sense. Dad was gone. Grandmommy died. Mom said we would be moving away from the only home I'd ever known, starting a new life, including a new school. I didn't understand why we were there, why this was happening to us. I didn't know what was going on. Mom didn't share anything with me. I wished I knew what was going on. I wished she would tell me. I felt so afraid, terrified. Were we going to be separated again?

I couldn't let on how afraid I felt; Mom liked me to be strong and brave. I could not let her see that I felt uncomfortable with so much uncertainty and change.

Although it had been five years, I could still smell the dog scent of the carpet we slept on. Mom and I never spoke of this incident once we moved to our own apartment in Santa Clara. Our silence was our way of leaving the pain in the past, never to be relived. Would we be homeless again? This could not be happening. I needed to make sure that we had a home; we could not be homeless again.

Elizabeth and I tried to maintain our friendship after we moved. But somehow, our lives just went on. We never spoke of this.

When I gave Mom my jar of money for rent, the painful past rushed to the surface. In the pit of my stomach, I knew I would not see this money again. I resigned myself to letting her have it and never asking about it.

I could work. I could make more money by picking up additional shifts. I could make enough to pay the rent. I knew I could keep Mom and me safe. I could also eat most of my meals at the restaurant. Grateful for the daily mistakes from the cooks and leftover inventory that would be thrown out at day's end, I had permission to take plenty of food home for me and Mom.

Chapter 15

The post delivery came; letters arrived from the colleges I applied to. Santa Clara University and San Francisco University logos donned the upper left corner of each envelope. My quivering fingers gently traced the names as I garnered the strength to read the contents. I should have waited for Mom. *Nah*, I thought, *I want to find out now, without her.* In case of bad news, I wanted the space to feel disappointment.

"It is our pleasure to welcome you to the graduating class of 1993," both letters read. Both: I had the choice of either school. I couldn't wait to go, to leave, to start my new adventure.

Elation turned to dread. All the money I earned had been used for rent and tuition; I had not saved anything for college. How would I pay for school? Without a scholarship, I wouldn't be able to attend either.

News of the college acceptances infused our home with a renewed energy of possibility, energy that Mom and I longed for.

"Santa Clara!" Mom cried. "You did it. We did it. You should go to Santa Clara; it's the best school. Jane's kids go there, and she says it's the best. And it's close to home, so you can stay here with me. This is a dream come true for me. I've worked so hard for this since you were a baby."

"I don't know yet, Mom," I said. "I'm still waiting on one final letter from Pepperdine."

I had applied to Santa Clara University to make Mom happy, but I wanted to leave my options open. No need to tell her. Once I got the other letters and had a plan to pay, I would tell her my decision. I smiled and put on a cheery, happy face. I didn't let on that I was considering going away to school.

Our high school had a great college acceptance rate. Our senior class was on pace for 100 percent college admissions. The principal had been on staff at SCU. News of my admission made him proud. Disheartened, I shared my deepest concerns about our family financial situation. He informed me of available financial aid personnel to contact in the event an athletic scholarship was not offered. I asked if he had any connections at San Francisco, but he did not. Disheartened, I had not heard back from Pepperdine. A sign of nonacceptance, I supposed.

My heart hurt as I signed a letter of intent to attend SCU in the fall of 1989. The elation on my mom's face was not enough to minimize the deep ache I felt, an ache that felt like I was cutting a part of me away.

I couldn't disappoint Mom. To hurt her was too much of a burden for me. She already shared the news with her friends, the proud mom she was. She already told anyone who would listen about my desire to become a doctor, explaining that I was attending SCU as a premed student to go to medical school. She had been through so much pain, endured so much hardship for me to receive my education. I could not leave now. I could not take this away from her. I could, however, make a deal to stay in the dorms. Although home was only three miles from campus, I needed some space. She agreed, easing my sullen heart.

Chapter 16

I thought I was in love with my best guy friend, Dominic. Back in freshman year, he had been the new kid, and we connected immediately. We shared sports and study hours. I just enjoyed his company and how he carried himself confidently, not like me when I had been the new kid. For three years, I harbored romantic thoughts. Every day, my feelings were harder to suppress. What if I said something careless and let it slip? Ugh. He had no idea.

Dominic's house was our favorite place to hang out. We could talk, study, and just be after school before practices. His house felt like home to me; his family was warm and welcoming. It was easy to be in his home, whether we were studying or watching television.

During the summer of 1988, before senior year began, our mutual group of friends enjoyed shenanigans by Dominic's pool. One day, after all our friends left, Dominic and I were alone, and I felt unusually nervous. This was not new. We spent so much time together as friends; why did I suddenly feel so weird? Dominic's reserve, for the first time, was palpable. He reached across the couch where we were sitting for my hand; he didn't speak. The awkwardness subsided as he leaned in to kiss me. The past three years of friendship culminated in this.

"Finally!" our friends all cried when they noticed us together the following day.

Senior year was set to be amazing.

Chapter 17

High school graduating class of 1989. The '80s generation inspired *Pretty in Pink*, *Sixteen Candles*, and *Breakfast Club*. The intersection of New Wave and Michael Jackson and Prince converged with Bon Jovi and Metallica to produce the greatest decade of music. We were gifted with music that captured the volatility of our hearts.

Senior year expectations were high as I straddled the line between my high school life, complete with honor classes, varsity sports, and working as many shifts, and my new world in college. I was comforted that Suzie and Dominic were attending colleges nearby; no one else from my senior class was attending SCU.

As June approached, the buzz of freedom rose. I was ready to graduate and felt done with high school. Not my friends, just the familiarity of the campus, the schedule, and the teachers. There was nothing more for me to learn, nowhere to expand. I had reached the ceiling. Maybe I was just done with my home life and Mom. I was ready to find out more about me, not just Arlette's daughter. I was infused with confidence in my cap and gown; I donned my full bravado suit to take on what was next. Mom and I had done everything possible to get me there. It was time.

No athletic scholarships were offered. However, I had applied for financial aid at SCU and was accepted. My principal suggested I take summer courses to prepare for the college curriculum. SCU's head basketball coach offered me the opportunity to try out as a walk-on in the fall. With that possibility, my intention was to prepare by doing the assigned workouts to make the team. Dominic and I planned to spend the summer together, playing on the court and preparing for our college years, still dating yet apart.

Dominic and I spent all of our free time together, on the basketball court and in the pool at his house. We were secure about our relationship as we prepared for college.

One day, just like every other day for the past four years at Dominic's house, I said goodbye to his family, and he walked me to my car. He kissed me goodbye, as he did every day. But on this day, his mother was watching us. I noticed her watching and felt flustered as I drove off in my car. An uncomfortable feeling was brewing in my heart.

With my car windows open, I could see her disapproving glare. Her piercing blue eyes let me know that she was displeased by what she witnessed. The energy emanating from her was unmistakable. Humiliation rose up through my body. Although I knew we didn't do anything wrong, I was filled with a burning sensation of shame. I didn't understand what I was feeling, but it seemed familiar. It was the same shame I felt when I started skating at the new ice rink. I didn't know what it meant, but I knew I had to get out of there, now.

I had planned to meet Dominic the next day at the courts; I was uncertain of what he would say. I cried at what I suspected was to come.

The next day, Dominic looked like he had not slept; his eyes were puffy, face swollen. He was there yet not really there. Making no mention about yesterday's confrontation with his mother, I went about our time together as if nothing happened. The heavy silence weighed on us; no words were appropriate in this moment. I said goodbye and added that he could just call me later. I left, saying nothing else, hurting too much to formulate any coherent sentences that could adequately describe the garbled mess of feelings squeezing my heart.

At one point while we worked out, Dominic threw the ball to me with more force than necessary. He seemed agitated by our new, unknown status. Uncertain of what to say or how to act, not wanting to ask about the conversation between him and his mom, I threw the ball back at him with more force than either of us expected. He threw the ball back at me; I took it and walked slowly through the drill, purposely messing up my footwork and missing the shot at the end, with complete indifference.

He finally boiled over at my willful disregard for the drills he designed to help me make the team in the fall; his anger came to surface.

"You have a chance to play in college," he said, "and I don't. And here you are, being lazy and not even willing to try. You don't know how lucky you are to be going to SCU. You are wasting your chance."

My tears welled up; I had never heard Dominic direct his temper at me. I had only seen him angry a few times, and it was never at me. His consistent temperament was one quality I loved about him. I had seen him upset, never like this, not at me.

"With both of us going to different colleges soon," I replied coolly, "maybe this is a good time for us to separate and spend some time apart. It's probably better for us to go on in our own directions, where we are free to make new friends."

Did I really say that out loud? I wanted to take every word back, to undo the damage I knew I caused by the look of dejection on Dominic's face.

The words repeated in my mind all the way to my car. Was this really how we were ending? What happened? I had walked off the court without saying a word, stunned by my own words.

Maybe he just needed time to cool off and then he would call me. In a few days, in a week. Once his anger settled down, we could just talk.

But he never called. I felt guilty about my behavior but was unable to dial his number, no matter how many times I picked up the phone. My heart knew: I screwed up. I just couldn't allow myself to think about what I had done. This couldn't be; what a fucking idiot I was.

As I replayed our argument, I went back to the day his mother saw us. She was so furious. She looked at me in a way I didn't understand then; it all happened so fast. As I thought about the events of that day, I was certain about what I felt.

Could it be true that as long as Dominic and I were just schoolmates, his parents would welcome me into their home? But the moment they knew we were more than friends, I was no longer welcome?

Anguish squeezed my heart with such force, I thought my heart would stop beating at any moment. I was despondent by how badly I screwed up my relationship with Dominic; there was no recovering from the damage I inflicted on us. I would not even know how. I could not tell him how I felt or what I was thinking. If he didn't want to call me, then I would let his choice be. I was hurting and didn't know how to make the pain go away. I couldn't make it stop.

Fuck, this was not how it was supposed to be. This was not the way my plan worked. I worked twice as hard to deflect unwanted attention from me. I followed all the rules and never did anything bad or wrong.

I became a good student and a good athlete, and I was accepted to a good college. I followed all the rules; I blended in so no one would know, so no one would find out. I made sure to smile and was happy all the time. I made sure to never mention any part of my childhood, as if I could wipe it away in one swipe of the eraser. I made sure the darkness of my childhood wouldn't seep through to my new life. I left me in San Jose when we left.

I couldn't escape. I couldn't hide, as hard as I tried. I really wasn't good enough. I didn't really fit in. I still wasn't good enough to be accepted. Maybe it was for the best that I was going to a new school in the fall. No other student from my class was attending SCU. No one would know me there. This was a chance for me to start over and put high school behind me. It was time to move on, just as I had six years earlier when we left San Jose. I could start over again.

That night, I went to work at the restaurant; my circle of friends were there.

"Yes, I want a shot," I told them after work. "What is it? Okay."

As my lips turned numb and my words slurred, my aching heart faded into the background.

I liked having a separate life at work, a circle of friends where I was free to be different. There was no need to be an overachiever, an insecure college-bound girl. I was free to stop following the stringent rules, free to get drunk and pass out at their house, at least for the rest of the summer.

PART 2

Chapter 18

The dorm's elevator cables felt as shaky as my decision to attend Santa Clara University. My nerves frayed when the doors open on the seventh floor; I was glad to bring my belongings into my room before the flood of students rushed to get settled in. I questioned my choice to reside in the eleven-story dorm, the most social building on campus.

My new roommate would be there any moment. Though we spoke on the phone a few times, I would be relieved when we met. I arrived in our designated room, located just to the left as I exited the elevator. With the door open, I guardedly smiled at every student passing by. One stopped in front of the door and looked at the number and then glanced at me.

"Are you Natacha?" she said. "It's me, Daisy."

I hugged her, any anxieties melting away. Our energies connected instantly as we scouted the campus layout. We planned our meal schedules so we could meet up between our classes on the opposite ends of campus.

I had the prerequisite freshman biology major's schedule: Biology 101, Chemistry 101, English Literature. At the end of the first week of class, I thought, *Oh, fuck. I'm in trouble. I should have taken summer classes; it seems everyone else here did. It's going to be okay. No need to panic, yet. Remember, this is how you felt when you started at your new junior high school. Who cares if most of the dorm attended some amazing private schools?*

The sound of Daisy's voice brought me back to the syllabi on my lap.

"My classes seem really hard too," she said. "As long as we go to all of our classes and study hard, I think we'll be okay."

The kindness and confidence in Daisy's voice gave me the courage to open my notebooks to review the day's class notes.

Basketball tryouts were in three weeks, and volleyball was next week. I wished I felt the confidence to match the courage I needed to attend. I needed to be on a team, either team, any team, which forced me to show up. I had to be on a team. Sports was my way of coping with life, which felt unmanageable. Being on a team was my way to survive. I had to earn a spot on a team to feel like I could endure.

During the first week of volleyball tryouts, I thought, *Who am I kidding? I don't have the skills or the athletic ability to keep up, let alone compete with these girls. There is no way I would be selected.* Despondent by the outcome of volleyball, I hoped for a better outcome with basketball, having been personally invited by the coach. I perked up.

My enthusiasm to be selected for basketball crashed after I met the other hopefuls at the first open gym workout with the team. My abilities were not even close. Dejected and sullen, I walked back to my dorm room. If I had a tail, it would have been between my legs, announcing to the world the shameful performance at tryouts.

When I got back to the dorm, one of my floormates said, "Hey, I'm headed to work out with the crew team later; want to join me?"

"What's the crew team?" I asked.

"The rowing team," she explained. "There's a big group heading over. Everyone is welcome."

"Sure," I said, perking up again. "Sounds like fun."

I knew nothing about crew or rowing, but I went along for the social connection and to meet some new girls to work out with. At that moment, I needed something good.

Chapter 19

"There are no tryouts," the crew coach explained. "This is an open invitation to all of you who think you have what it takes to be a member of the rowing team. We will meet here every afternoon for workouts. There are sixty-two of you here today. By the end of the week, ten of you will drop out. By Christmas break, another twenty will have quit. By the first race in March, whoever is still here will be on the team to represent SCU. We need sixteen rowers to fill two boats."

"I don't get it," I said. "As long as we show up to practice and do the workouts, we're on the team?"

"If you make it through the workouts and want to stay," the coach said, "you are guaranteed a spot on the team; you will race."

Wow, I thought. *I'm on a team.*

I didn't care that we met at five o'clock in the morning for conditioning, and had practice at seven in the morning on Saturdays, and then met again at four o'clock weekdays in the weight room. I could do it. The coach gave us individual personalized workouts based on our current ability; all I needed to do was follow it. Yes, I could do this.

I'd never followed such a rigorous workout schedule. A sense of ownership and pride for my body developed as I experienced myself becoming an athlete. While we pretended to moan and groan at the

5 a.m. start, secretly, I loved it. I loved the satisfaction of the changes my body was going through.

Daisy liked me to wake her so she could study before any shenanigans began in the dorm. Her commitment to studying reminded me of Elizabeth. I envied her dedication. I studied after class, between work shifts at Sizzler, and after workouts, but only until nine o'clock, to ensure quality sleep for the following day's workout. They were getting harder and more intense every week. My commitment to the workouts garnered the coach's attention, as my rowing time on the machine got faster, and I was consistently one of the top three rowers. I knew with complete certainty that I would not quit. Nothing would get me to quit.

Finals were next week already. With our final official team practice of the year, Coach was on target with his predictions. Roughly thirty of us participated in organized team workouts as we discussed holiday expectations and cautions about class schedules when we returned in January.

I needed as much time as possible to prepare for finals. Without team meetings or work hours, I was confident I'd have enough study hours. I was moderately prepared as I walked into finals, and my inadequate study habits resulted in my turning in the last exam paper in each class.

Concerned about my grades but happy to be done, I returned home. Our grades would be mailed prior to the start of the next semester.

Home was more comfortable for Mom and me. With workouts and work, the holidays this year were lighter, more enjoyable, less encumbered by Mom's critical eye. She was pleased with the direction my life was going.

The grades arrived: disbelief. Complete and total shock. Two Cs and a D in chemistry. A failing 1.8 grade point average. I knew I was struggling with the course work but had no idea I was that far behind.

I was disappointed but not completely disheartened. I knew there was room for me to improve. I knew I hadn't applied myself to the best of my ability. I knew I let myself down with my study habits. With the rowing team, a few parties, working, and social time in the dorms, I had slacked off from the diligent effort that earned my grades in high school. Once I got back to better discipline, my grades would improve. I was simply overwhelmed in the beginning, with so many changes. I knew I'd be okay.

Chapter 20

The beauty of the sunrise over the waterway at five o'clock was diminished by the foul stench of garbage in the water. This waterway connected the undeveloped land of Silicon Valley up to the San Francisco Bay. Some mornings, the odor so thick and foul, it formed a coat lining the back of my throat; I could still taste the rancid particles when I was in class.

Coach's predictions once again were on point. The remaining twenty of us competed for top coveted seats in the boat. Teams were based on individual weight and our time trails. The maximum weight to qualify on race day as a lightweight division was 129 pounds. If overweight, rowers were assigned to the open class. At 140 pounds, there was a possibility I could be on the faster, lightweight team. I already shed twenty pounds since the beginning of the school year and trusted that I could lose ten more pounds by March.

I carried a lot of clout when I walked into classes wearing the coveted maroon, white, and black rowing jacket. Only twenty of us had earned the right to wear one. The uniform overshadowed any remaining inadequacies of the 1.8 GPA from the previous quarter. Infused with admiration and respect emanating from the other students' eyes, I took a seat in class.

A more disciplined routine this quarter propelled me to maintain my demanding schedule of double workouts, coursework, and weekend shifts in the restaurant. The dorm-floor antics had subsided, and social gatherings were minimal; studying was more serious now for everyone.

I took a practical, pragmatic approach to my schedule and my life; I completed the quarter as intended. Well, almost.

My grade point average was now 2.25.

What the fuck? I thought. *I actually worked hard this quarter. I felt really good about the effort I dedicated to my course work. What was I missing? Why wasn't I getting better grades?*

I was studying as hard as I could. Daisy and my teammates seemed to have adjusted just fine; their grades markedly improved from the fall. I didn't really have time to figure this out. Our first race was in two weeks. I was out of the academic critical zone. Over the summer, I would create a better solution. Right now, I was still five pounds over the lightweight limit; the weight was becoming increasingly difficult to shed.

I was disappointed and pissed at myself; my first ever race, and I would be rowing in the open weight class. It was okay, but not as competitive as the lightweight. For the amount of effort I put into training, the open class was not acceptable.

I couldn't celebrate with the girls I trained with; I had pushed to shave seconds off our time trails, but I felt separated from them in the medal ceremony. Not being with them disgusted me; I promised myself to race with them in two weeks.

"Don't worry," my teammates said. "You'll be with us next race. We'll help you drop the last few pounds; we promise you will make weight next time."

131. 130. 129. 130. 131. 129. Teetering on the edge before race day. My teammates were counting on me for this, as was I. Our training and time trials were amazingly fast these past two weeks. We knew we had a great team and a chance to win. I didn't want to disappoint myself or them. I needed to make weight. I had to make weight, no matter what.

"Drink only coffee for two days before the race," one teammate offered.

"But I'll feel really tired if I don't eat at all," I objected.

"Then just don't eat an entire twenty-four hours before weigh-in, then eat before the race," another suggested.

"Okay, I hope it'll be enough," I mumbled below my breath.

"Or just do what we all do," a third said, clearly annoyed by the entire conversation.

"What do you mean?" I asked.

They shared furtive glances, informing me I would not like their suggestion.

"Just eat enough to make it through workouts. If you eat too much, go to the bathroom, stick your finger in your throat, and make yourself throw up. On race day, don't eat or drink anything until after weigh-in. Then you can eat whatever you want to give you the energy to win."

Horrified, disgusted, but relieved, I followed their advice and weighed in at 128, guaranteeing my spot in the lightweight boat. My teammates and I celebrated our victory. Making weight that season was never a problem again.

Chapter 21

When I moved out of the dorm, I opted for the stairwell, allowing me to circumvent the chaotic energy of everyone saying goodbye. Freshman year had come to an end; I couldn't get out of there fast enough. The seven-story dorm I once felt joy to call home was now just a concrete building, shaming me about who I had become in the nine months. The person I morphed into now felt like a cheater in sport and an academic failure. I was relieved to be home, where I could stop the whirlwind of confusion. The quiet space of my own room offered solace.

I found comfort in the familiarity of the restaurant; the routine of work helped me feel grounded again. Without impending weigh-ins, my one workout each day felt revitalizing, enjoyable. My summer routine was simple, unencumbered.

The ease of summer, familiar friends at the restaurant, and a new circle of friends at the gym rebooted my soul. Refreshed, I stayed calm and felt able to begin a new school year. The shame of my weight control tactics motivated me to learn about nutrition; I discovered how to eat properly, as an athlete. My body changed; it got stronger. I was leaner and healthier. My spirit was also lighter; there was even a spring in my step, as a new beau entered my world.

Daisy and I agreed to room together again; our familiar energy soothed me as we moved into the smaller dorm. I appreciated the quietness; the freshman chaos was gone.

I took organic chemistry and physics. I was more prepared as I calmly stared at the daunting schedule. The familiarity of school life provided confidence to reset my academic path. I was undecided about participating on the rowing team this year; I attended the first team meeting, just to see.

Although team workouts would be challenging, practices would not begin for another two months for returning members. This news pushed me from undecided to a definite yes. The schedule was manageable for me to participate without compromising myself academically. Feeling encouraged by my fortitude to maintain a more balanced and disciplined schedule of work, workouts, boyfriend, and homework, sophomore year began.

The certainty I felt as the year began burst with the reality of my midterm grades. To my dismay, my best efforts were only good enough for barely passing marks. I knew I could do better than that. I would just get up earlier and stay up later to do more before finals. I even found vitamins at the local health food shop that helped me stay awake and focused. Because they were natural, I gave no second thought to taking six pills per day. It was what the athletes at the gym were also consuming, so it must have been okay.

I felt good about finals. I believed my extra study hours made a difference. After the tests, I was ready for Christmas vacation and headed home for the four-week break.

When the grades arrived, I nervously opened the letter. I feel nervous, although I had no reason to. There was no report, just a letter from my academic advisor, asking to see me before classes began.

I headed to the school; the administration building felt cold. This was my first time in here, and I promised myself it would be the last.

"Ms. Nelson," he began, "you are on academic probation. You need to make academics your priority this quarter in order to avoid failing out. I suggest you quit the rowing team and focus on your studies."

Quit? I thought. *I can't quit the team.* Saying nothing, I just smiled and nodded in agreement to the advisor, accepting that I must rearrange my priorities. With the rowing season training now set to begin, I needed to make some changes. I decided to cut back on my hours at Sizzler.

Without my job and without a boyfriend, my school schedule just opened up. I knew I should quit the team, but I liked being on the team. I need to be on the team; it was all I had there in school. Being on the team was all I had; it made me feel like I was a part of something. I couldn't quit now; I worked too hard to get there.

Academic probation? Oh, fuck. What happened? I thought I had it all under control. I was losing control of my life. I could feel rage, anxiety, and confusion all swirling inside. The pressure was squeezing me so hard, I needed to let it out. I needed to let go. The pressure hurt me so much; I didn't know how to contain it anymore. I didn't know what to do or how to make it stop.

Ice cream subdued the pressure. French fries suppressed the anxiety. Cookies made the shame go away. The rush of a euphoric high completely took over once I threw it all up. The pressure finally stopped.

Sitting in class, I felt numb, like an intruder in a world where I didn't belong. I was a fraud, on academic probation. I guessed I was not as smart as I thought. I was not as smart as everybody wanted me to be: Mom, my high school teachers, the principal, myself. This was my last chance, my only chance. I had to figure this out. I had to figure out my life before it was too late.

I could not quit the team. It was the only place I felt normal, the only place I didn't feel like a loser or a fraud. I knew I could not continue with the intensity of the team workouts and training and keep up with my schoolwork. Being on the team was too important to me, but I didn't need to work so hard to be the best. I didn't need to prove my ability to compete, I just needed to stay on the team, stay with my team. As long as my weight remained below 129, I could stay. I could go to our morning practices and then skip afternoon workouts; most of the team worked out on their own, anyway. I would just say I'll go alone so I can make it to study groups, which was half-true. As long as I could perform at team practices and keep my weight down, I would be able to compete in the spring.

Controlling my weight was difficult. I liked to eat when I studied. Food minimized anxiety. Sugar kept me awake and able to focus. Eating soothed me. Food calmed me. It made me feel everything would be okay. Eating made the scary world feel less scary. It distracted me from the uncomfortable resentment, anger, and rage that keeps showing up. Resentment and rage had become constant companions. I couldn't seem to get rid of them. Food made them go away, at least for a little while.

Food made the sadness go away. It made the loneliness go away. It made all of the feelings go away. Losing control of my weight, I could feel panic coming over me. I no longer just purged before a competition weigh-in. As my food intake increased to squelch the rise of uncomfortable feelings, the need to purge increased to maintain control over my weight.

Numb to the disgusting feelings of binging and purging, I replaced disgust with shame, shame for what I was doing. Shame for who I had become. I felt a soothing, familiar comfort when I ate and then felt high after I purged. The release gave my brain a physical release, a release like a pressure valve. I felt drugged, yet clear. I was calm and able to concentrate. I felt normal. At least for a while, until the next waves of shame, humiliation, and guilt crept back, and I needed to make them go away, the only way I knew how.

Chapter 22

The rowing season came and went with no fanfare. My teammates and I won a few races and placed well in others. I felt no enjoyment of the events. I felt no excitement with my teammates. I felt nothing. I made sure I'd feel nothing. I went to class, studied, worked out. The hours of my days were consumed with making sure I had my favorite foods on hand to numb all of the uncomfortable feeling vying for positioning at the front of my mind. By now, I spent more time at home than in the dorm; there were fewer eyes on me, less chance of being caught. Whatever leftover energy remained, I used for school.

Aware of my inability to catch up, I decided to drop organic chemistry to ensure a passing grade for the quarter. After my dismal 2.0 GPA from fall quarter, I needed at minimum the same to continue. The 1.8 GPA for winter showed me I had not been successful.

The spring quarter and my sophomore year ended. With the rowing season complete, desperate to regain some sense of normalcy, I went back to work at the restaurant, where I felt safe. It was my last chance to do right, my last chance to find a way out of the mess I created. I finished the school year commuting from home; I felt no desire to engage with anyone on campus. I was completely disconnected, disengaged from my life. I finished my finals and moved my personal belongings out of the dorm room late one night, not saying goodbye to anyone.

Lost, I went back to work full time at the restaurant.

The letter with the Santa Clara University logo arrived. There was dread in the pit of my stomach, so far from the elation I felt when I got the acceptance letter, which now seemed like a lifetime ago.

I unfolded the letter and read, "Due to your failure to maintain the minimum academic required GPA …"

I didn't read the entire letter. I didn't need to. For the second consecutive quarter, my GPA was 1.8. I had officially flunked out. I was officially a college failure.

Congratulations, Tash, I thought, *you really are as stupid as you thought. Now, everyone will know the truth. You are now the loser you were trying so hard to hide. You cannot hide the disgrace and shame of who you are anymore. You knew better than to believe you could fit in at a school like Santa Clara University. What a disgrace you've become.*

Chapter 23

What could I say to Mom? How should I tell her? How could I explain this failure? How could I face her and see the disappointment in her eyes when I told her I failed? I couldn't really explain the circumstances to her; I didn't really understand how this all happened. The two years were a blur. I'd just wait for the right time, a better time, just not right now, not yet.

Work would buy time through the summer to come up with a plan before she had to know. Feeling restless and useless, I added a second serving job to my schedule. I needed to stay busy. Time alone with my mind was a miserable choice of company. The incessant chatter: *College dropout, flunked out of school; your life is waiting tables. This is what you have to look forward to. Your college friends are getting summer intern jobs, working their way toward their career. You really screwed up. There is no way to fix this mess. You don't get a second chance.* The voices in my head were so loud. Only food made them stop. Only food silenced the voices, even if only for a few hours. The voice of shame that food does not silence, alcohol does.

At work, I knew how to turn on the charm, smile, flash my dimples, and have light hearted, superficial conversations about nothing. I smiled and kept on smiling. Smiling kept people engaged, yet not too close. Too close, they might find out the truth. I could not allow the truth to be exposed. I had to keep my secret; no one could find out. If I pretended I was fine, if I pretended my life was great, if I pretended I was still in school and covered up the lies with a bright smile, then I would be okay.

Every morning, I started my day with a cup of coffee and a slice of toast. I worked out, and for the entire morning, I felt normal. Every day, I woke up and promised myself today would be the day I made it through the entire day without binging and purging. Every day I worked a lunch shift, I could complete most of the day without incident. If I had a dinner shift, I knew for those hours, I would be comfortable and safe.

Once home, I tried to dodge Mom's inquiring eyes. The way she looked at me, I thought she knew. I scampered off to my room before she could ask about my plans. If I stopped to talk with her, she would find out. In my room, I heard her walk past my door. I remembered when I wanted nothing more than for Mom to come into my room to hug me good night. Now I prayed she walked by.

I was so far removed from the high school girl who stayed up to study, with Mom coming in to kiss me good night. My heart hurt as I closed my eyes, remembering the cookies and the look of pride she had for me.

One night, I heard her footsteps pause at my door. "Good night," she whispered through my closed door.

"Good night, Mom," I replied; when I heard her bedroom door close, I made my way down the stairs.

I made myself a plate of nachos and turned on the television to see what was on. So much for making it through the day; another broken promise to myself.

Tomorrow will be better, I thought. *Tomorrow will be different. It has to be.*

Mom and I were on different paths. She just started her own business: floral designs, primarily for weddings and special occasions. She was truly a gifted florist; I was so proud of her, finally recognizing her talent and making her American dream come true. Mom was a survivor. I wished I had her survival instincts. She hustled to do whatever necessary to get her business growing and profitable. All five feet of her. Arlette was feisty and sometimes a bully. She was a gutsy fighter in life, for sure. We could not be more different.

"What classes will you be taking this fall?" she asked me one day. My coffee spilled on the counter. *Shit*, I thought. *She ambushed me; what do I say? The truth? Not now; I'm not ready for this conversation just yet.*

"I'm going to take a quarter off," I said. "I'm going to work through the holidays and then go back in January. I feel burned out from school and just need a break."

My gaze remained on the floor; I dared not make eye contact with Mom.

"Okay," she replied.

I was grateful she opted not to pursue the conversation.

I rushed upstairs to get out of the way; my reflection in the hallway mirror stopped me. Usually, I hurried to put on makeup and brush my hair. This morning, I stopped. Something grabbed my attention.

My eyes looked sunken in, surrounded by dark puffy patches. My cheeks were swollen. My skin had an ashy hue to it, no longer my mocha-caramel, bronzed tone. Running my fingers through my hair, I could feel the clumps of hair coming out. I looked sick. I was sick. Weighing in at 121 pounds, my feelings matched how I looked. If I could see it, I knew others must have noticed too. No one asked, so I didn't tell. I put on my size 2 clothes and began my day.

At work, I had a purpose: take care of customers and provide excellent service. No work required, no hard thinking involved. I showed up, focused on their needs, and forgot about mine. I enjoyed my work. I enjoyed the exchanges with customers, hearing about their work, being a part of a first date or a business meeting. Caring for customers helped me feel human. I had a sense of pride and dignity in what I did. I felt good about myself when people were inspired to share their day with me.

While I worked, I felt like a normal human being. I forgot that I was an addict. I felt needed, wanted, useful. For those hours, to those customers, I was not a failure. I was not worthless. I was not a disappointment.

My smile faded when I left the restaurant. Leaving my purpose and dignity behind, I went to the gym and then home. I was trapped in my destructive cycle; I didn't know how to get out.

Chapter 24

One morning, I was awakened for the third day in a row by an irregular, rapid heartbeat. I was terrified that my heart would stop.

I knew something was wrong. I knew my heart rate was not normal. If I didn't get help soon, I believed I could actually die. I didn't want to die. I needed help. For six months, I unsuccessfully tried to break this addiction on my own.

I opened the phone book to therapists and made an appointment with a doctor specializing in eating disorders.

Our fifty-minute hour left no time for small talk. At ninety dollars an hour, I had to get the help I needed in two or three sessions; that was all I could afford.

"How long have you been binging and purging?" the doctor asked.

"Over a year," I replied. "Almost two."

"Tell me about your dad. What is your relationship with him like?"

My dad? I thought. *Why the fuck is he asking about my dad? I have an eating disorder. I need help. My dad has nothing to do with this. I have not seen or spoken to him since high school freshman basketball season. Fuck no. I'm not talking about my dad; he's dead to me.*

"We are not close," I answered. "There's nothing to talk about there."

"Do you see your father?"

What is with this fucking therapist? I already told him; there's nothing to talk about regarding my father.

"I don't have a father. He hasn't been a part of my life since I was ten. Can we move on to what's important here? I need help, and my father is not the issue. Can you help me or not?"

"I don't think I am the right therapist for you."

I was ashamed of my behavior; my outburst surprised me. Terrified and disheartened, I went home, pulled the covers over my head, and fell asleep. I didn't know what else to do or where else to go.

God, I thought, *I don't really believe in you, but please help.*

Awakened by the sun's intensity through my window, I realized it'd been sixteen hours since I crumbled into bed. It was ten o'clock; the morning was almost gone. Having already missed my morning workout and late to start my shift at work, I called in sick. I felt the need to just slow down today.

The drowsy pace of the morning alleviated the sense of disruption of my daily routine. I felt calm, although I didn't know why. Nothing in my life had changed; nothing was different.

Coffee in hand, I open the *Metro*, our local paper. Dedicated to sports and entertainment, I turned to see what movies were playing. A matinee, alone, sounded good.

Flipping through the pages of light reading, my eyes locked on an advertisement on the bottom of the page:

"Stanford University looking for women to participate in a one-year study on eating disorders. Free treatment for those selected. Please call for more information."

The God I didn't believe in had my attention. I started to cry. The kind of cry that invoked my entire body. The kind of cry that once started, the only way to stop was to cry all the way through to the end. So that was exactly what I did: I cried. Then I called the number in the ad.

"The study is a full year," the woman who answered the phone said. "Are you able to commit for an entire year?"

"Yes, I know I can."

"You can only miss two sessions, then you will be dismissed. Are you sure?"

My resounding yes took my breath away.

I need to be a part of this study. This was my second, my only, my last chance. I didn't know what I did to deserve this. I didn't think God was listening. I still wasn't sure I believed in him but I promised not to blow this opportunity.

Chapter 25

A palliative balm spread through my body as I sat on my bed, reviewing the structured study schedule. An overwhelming sense of awe filled my heart. Help at last; help was here. I knew I would be okay.

Sessions with the therapist focused on food habits and my life. With minimal interjections about my father, I was able to relax and answer the questions completely. Hearing the honesty in my account of the details, I sat back in the chair; I could hardly believe the direction my life had taken.

I was comforted by the therapist's lack of reaction. She was able to sit and listen to the accounts of my failures without condemning me. I shared more and more. Her warm demeanor was soothing but not enough for me to respond to the emotionally charged questions about my father. I wasn't ready yet. I didn't think I'd ever be ready to face my past. I'd pushed my memories of my father so far down, I didn't want to retrieve them. I buried him for good a long time ago.

How did I get so far off track? I asked myself. *This was not my plan; how did I go wrong?* My questions went unanswered.

Entering the second month of treatment, I freely reported that my binge-purge episodes had decreased; progress.

"Tell me about your future plans," the therapist said.

This was the first mention of future; therapy had been about the past up through then.

A desperate yearning for school tugged at my heart every day. Shame pushed the sensation back down.

"I flunked out of college," I said. "There's no way for me to go back now."

Hearing my voice utter the words, humiliation traveled through me. She was sweet, telling me I could go back to school. I supposed it was her job, to encourage me to believe I could do anything. I used to believe that too. I didn't anymore. All I ever wanted was to study to human body, to be a doctor. There was no way of coming back to my dream now; not ever.

"I am oddly fascinated by how my mind got me to this point," I admitted. "How did I end up here, in this position? My interest is piqued, not for my recovery, but for my own understanding."

"If you're interested in psychology," she suggested, "would you be interested in reading on your own, instead of going to classes?"

My posture straightened up at the idea. "Yes," I said.

"I'm sure you can find a few books that capture your interest. You can even try the local college bookstores for used books."

"The junior college is on my way home; I'll stop in their bookstore."

"That's great; just walk around their bookstore and see whatever interests you. Let me know how it goes at our next session."

My body could feel the stabbing pain of guilt, shame, and humiliation coursing through my heart, with each step on campus. Walking through the bookstore, I was aware of the fact that it had been over a year since I attended any class.

In line to purchase a few books, I could not take my eyes off a course catalog. The cashier asked if I would like a copy.

"Sure, why not?" I said with a tone of indifference that did not completely match how I was feeling.

Outside the bookstore, I flipped through the pages. I intended to discard the catalogue; one less thing to carry to my car. I reached for the trash bin and stepped onto the mat leading to the registrar's office; the door opened.

As the door opened inward, I felt ushered into the lobby, unable to stay out. I felt frozen, standing in the lobby, and then my legs began to move. One step in front of the other; my feet stopped at the registration desk.

"Are you a new or returning student?" the clerk asked.

"Um, I'm not sure," I replied. "I'm new here, but I used to go to SCU."

"What classes do you want to sign up for?"

I heard a voice speaking, but it was not mine. It came from my mouth, but I didn't recognize it,

"Beginning psychology."

"Okay, we have an opening. Is there anything else?"

"Can I take an anatomy class?"

"Yes, Anatomy and Physiology 101 is available."

"I'll take that too."

"Welcome to college; classes begin a week from Monday."

I was confused by my behavior; some part me just signed up to go back to school. A part of me, a familiar stranger, peered out from under the cloak of guilt and signed us up for classes. She had an idea and a plan. I thought I liked her. I was not sure what she was doing, but I'd go along with her, at least for now.

"Maybe she is the part of you that still dreams of becoming a doctor," my therapist suggested; her jubilation at my news was the most emotion she'd expressed since we began working together.

"Well, she can keep on dreaming," I said. "I just don't want to feel disappointed by some grand plan that has no way of becoming real."

I secretly held onto her words; a spark in me wished for the impossible to become real.

College was familiar, yet different. Sitting in class, taking notes with my assortment of colored pens, I felt human again. The discipline of two classes, working, studying, workouts, and therapy felt like just the right amount. I passed midterms with two As; slowly, I could feel the warmth of my own dignity returning.

As therapy began to conclude, school classes continued. Life felt manageable. There was some uncertainty, but it was not uncomfortable; the stability of school slowly filled the void in my soul. By the end of the school year, my goal of becoming a doctor no longer seemed completely unreasonable.

Once again, my other self showed up unexpectedly. This time, she dialed the phone and made an appointment for us.

"These are the required courses," the advisor explained. "If completed as scheduled, and we have the necessary paperwork, you'll be eligible to begin in March. Welcome to Palmer College of Chiropractic."

Chapter 26

Sitting in my first chiropractic class, I remembered my first experience of being adjusted when I was fourteen. It was part of my routine with Mom. Before a treatment, I would get a buzzing and ringing in my ears; after an adjustment, they would go away, and I always slept better on those nights.

The schedule was overwhelming and daunting. Classes and accompanying labs were eight hours each day. I was taking thirty-six units per quarter, for the next three years. I wasn't sure if I could keep up with this rapid moving pace. I felt some confidence in my ability to study, to keep with up with these demands, but doubt creeped in as the days proceeded.

I no longer thought of myself as dumb or stupid. I knew my style and pace of learning. I liked to take time to digest material, all of it. I made sure to read and fully understand the intricate hows and whys of the body's mechanics and functions. Information needed to marinate in my mind. Once assimilated, I could visualize the smallest particle and the grand structure simultaneously. As a visual leaner, I took notes in colored pencils. Pictures of human organs and systems, down to the tiniest of cells, were retained in memory in full color. In unison, the swirling movements acted as guides to interpret and make sense of the dance of the entire network of the human body.

My way of learning was effective for recalling and understanding intricate information that is often invisible. However, it was not conducive to the structured curriculum. I always knew this about myself. Back in junior high school, I could recall seemingly useless minutia after taking notes in color.

In my first college courses, class outlines were printed and handed out so the instructor could move along at a faster pace. I didn't understand that; my way of taking notes was a vital part of my way of learning. My brain was able to use colors to create visuals in my mind. My way works, but it's slower.

Sitting in class, I was overwhelmed by the copious amount of information disseminating at once. I loved the subject matter. Every fiber of my being danced with joy as I made the connection of all the parts of the body. I enjoyed the intensity and depth of the science, combined with the psychology of the mind and the philosophy of human design. I was willing to stay up all night, quit my job, and do whatever necessary to keep up in class.

Every curiosity for learning about the human body was being fulfilled. I knew, without any doubt, this was exactly the work I was supposed to be doing. My second grade self knew I wanted to become a doctor. And here I was: a rough start, but finally on track to fulfill my dreams.

Studying for midterms and finals felt like triage. Although I passed, checking the results brought to the surface the familiar discomfort as grades were posted on the common wall; although posted by class number, everyone could see the entire class grades. Based on the results, I was one of the few having a difficult time.

I feared that my classmates would find out I was the one with the lowest grade; I was less outgoing, less interested in social gatherings with other students. I withdrew from other students in effort to conceal myself. I want to remain inconspicuous in hopes my grades would not identify me.

I still felt like a fraud. My past made me feel like I didn't really deserve to be there. Being a recovering addict meant I was less capable of success. Failing out of school for an addiction meant there was something wrong with me, rendering me unfit to work in health care. I kept my head down, stayed to myself, and did my best to blend in. I wanted to hide, to not draw any attention to myself for any reason.

Just blend in, I thought. *Stay unnoticed. Don't talk unless spoken to. Don't engage in any conversation so that you don't let any of your past slip out. They can't do anything to you if they don't know. No one can ever find out. If they do, it will be the end.*

I kept my head down; first quarter, done. Kept my head down; second quarter complete. It was working; my plan was working. No one knew; no one would find me out.

When the fourth quarter's results were posted, I looked at the sheet and thought, *Oh, fuck. My first failing grade.* I had made through the third quarter without a hitch. But there it was, right there for everyone to see. I was not the only one who didn't pass the class, but that didn't matter. I was the only one with a secret to hide.

I started the fourth quarter on a special schedule; I repeated the class with the class below me. This was familiar, much like algebra with my khaki skirt standing out in the sea of navy blue. No longer inconspicuous, I felt exposed, vulnerable for others to judge. *That's the girl who flunked:* I can hear them in my mind, laughing at me.

What if I was found out? What would happen to me if my secret was exposed? I thought they knew. If they didn't, they would know soon. I was sure they were figuring it out. They looked at me like I didn't fit in. Who was I kidding? I was trying to hide my past, to pretend that my past didn't happen, to be something that I was not, someone I was not. I couldn't do it.

I was relieved when Christmas break arrived; I needed to figure out a plan, just in case. Just in case something went wrong when school started again, I needed a backup. What kind of job could I get now? Maybe I could get a job now that will give me security, a place where I could fit in. What else could I do that I was good at?

I had a lot of friends who worked on the police and fire departments. Every day at the gym, at least one asked me when I was going to take the test for their city. I never took their offer seriously; I had plans of becoming a doctor. But now I was open to a new possibility, a possibility that seemed like a better fit for me. When I spoke with friends on the force, I was extremely confident I would be hired sooner rather than later.

I started the process, since getting hired can take a couple of years. I tested for all the local departments. I didn't want to go back to work at the restaurant. I didn't want to quit school; I could go on a modified schedule and take fewer classes, leaving me time to take law enforcement and fire safety classes. I continued to work out and prepared for the academy.

One day, the chief of police called me and offered me a job.

"Wow," I said. "Thank you, Chief."

I was not surprised to be hired, just that the process was complete in three months. I thought it would take longer.

"You will begin the Police Academy in June," he said.

Fuck yeah! My silent scream was masked by my casual smile. I didn't realize how valuable and wanted I could be to a department until this process. This was great.

Mom was overjoyed that I made a decision for work. Now that I had a job with benefits and security, she was elated. I could hear her in my head: *Finally, she is getting her act together. It is about time.*

Having an escape plan, I no longer cared about what my classmates knew; what they were saying was no longer of concern to me. I decide to finish classes at Palmer in June. I made sure to leave in good standing, just in case.

Chapter 27

My khaki uniform was perfectly pressed, with creases in just the right folds. My boots reflected the shine of the 101 degree sun beating on the asphalt. Police paraphernalia covered my uniform as I stood at attention for inspection. Hair in a tight bun, I certainly looked the part of a police officer. I was aware of my empty Glock .45. Every part of me appreciated the irony. I needed a handgun as a part of my duty to save my life, the life of a fellow officer, or that of a harmless civilian; I was conflicted by thoughts of taking a life, a human life, a human body, which I had such deep reverence for. I knew the intimate details of human development from conception and was aware of the life force in us; I was not yet sure I could do my job fully. Hopefully, with more training, I would develop more comfort. Attention to the smallest detail was the lesson of this drill, which was not lost on me.

Naturally, I gravitate to emergency medical training; my instincts were natural in this area. The lessons of officer safely also got my attention. I trained my eyes to have a new and different perspective on what was happening around me. I began to learn the lessons of discernment and navigated what I saw and trusted what I felt.

However, I was surprised by my intellectual desire to understand the nuances of the law. I felt a deep urge to dissect, discuss, and debate the law. I desired to verbally spar and articulate other sides of the law at once; I gained no favor with the training officers. I was contentious with one training officer and preferred to prove my point than to back down.

It was not my intention to be difficult or cause trouble. However, to me, the law had many sides that seemed open to interpretation, and I just didn't want to accept their view as the only version. That did not sit well in my gut. I felt the need to speak up and out. With my own experience with addiction, I could not buy into the belief that every addict was best served by incarceration. I used food; I could just have easily chose drugs. Food was simply more readily available for me.

There she was again: speaking out loud when I should have stayed quiet and gone along, but she just couldn't. I was still not sure who she was, but I was growing to like her more and more.

Approaching the halfway point of our academy training, I had a growing awareness of my discomfort for policework gnawing in my bones. I didn't love it the way my fellow cadets did. Although I was able to do the job, I didn't have the same love of it. I fit in with the people, but I didn't fit in with this particular service. What made me stay were the friendships and the camaraderie. Our navy blue uniforms were a powerful sign of the strength of our team. I miss being a part of a team; I couldn't leave this. I didn't want to leave this.

I'm not going to quit, I thought. *No way. I can't quit. I have no option but to stay. Mom is depending on this job for us. She needs me to keep this job. She needs us to have stability. I made a commitment to the department, to myself, to Mom. I have to stay. Time for me to grow up, put my big girl panties on, and get on with my life. Enough fucking around; grow up, already.*

The environment of rules and unquestioned procedures offered peace; there were policies and rules to follow each day. Those same rules suffocated, strangled, and imprisoned me.

I had to keep my mouth shut; as long as I stayed silent and did as I was instructed, I would be fine. I didn't want rock the boat or cause any disruptions. I no longer instigated confrontations with superiors. I stopped asking so many damn questions and drawing unwanted attention. This was no place to listen to my heart. This was a place to get my head on straight. Following my heart could get me reprimanded or killed. Listening to my heart would make me unlikable, unacceptable, and judged as difficult; that's no way to start a career in a field where promotions rely on being liked as much as aptitude.

My heart said to speak up and stay. My head reminded me of all the reasons why I needed this job. I chose to follow my head.

Six weeks until graduation. The intensity grew as our training involved more street scenarios. I came out of the locker room at 7:57. With growing sensation of discomfort, I stared at the clock as if it offered pertinent information I needed. Something felt off, yet I couldn't specify what was causing this feeling.

At 8:30, my presence was requested by my superiors. On the way to his office, he said, "Your inappropriate behavior in class yesterday goes against our policy and code of conduct."

That's odd, I thought to myself; my tactical training officer had specifically commented on how well I was deescalating situations. This was the first I heard of any misconduct. I hadn't witnessed or engaged in any inappropriate behavior. Naively, I walked into the interview room ready to offer any information.

Five hours later, I was unable to convince them I had done nothing wrong. Without solid evidence to substantiate their claims or my innocence, I appealed my case but it fell on deaf ears.

I needed a break and stood up. "I'm done," I said and walked out to disconnect from the ambush. I returned thirty minutes later, with a cooler head, attempting to resolve whatever misunderstanding was creating this confusion.

I was met with a shocking announcement:

"Your department feels you are a liability and is parting ways with you. They request that you go to their office and return their equipment. You're not being kicked out of the academy," he explained. "If you wish to continue and graduate, you will need to supply your own equipment. You can make up today's exams tomorrow. Good luck to you."

Without emotion, I walked out. No anger, no resentment, just emotionally flat. I felt nothing. Shock had turned to betrayal. I was completely unsuspecting. With no clear reasons or evidence, just like that, I lost my job. Replaying the conversation over and over, I tried to gain some insight or clarity through any nuance or inflection I could remember in their words and tones. Nothing.

Fuck that! my rage monster roared. Appearing with a vengeance the following morning, I vowed to finish the academy and get hired elsewhere. With the support of friends in other departments, they loaned me all the equipment I needed. Hearing of my grievance, a few even let me in on the dirty little secret: Not all officers look out for each other. Some are vindictive.

With their insight and support, I felt confident I would be hired again after graduation. For the final six weeks, my rage monster was on high alert. My protector would never again allow me to be caught off guard like I was. My rage monster, while vocally silent, expressed itself with full force. It propelled me, forcible staring at the training officers as I completed the course and graduated. I had a new appreciation for my friend named Rage. Rage got shit done. Rage didn't give a fuck if it was liked or not. I liked Rage. I thought I would keep Rage around with me for a while.

Mom was right; she said, "There will be people who don't like you and will purposely want to hurt you. You won't know who they are, and you won't know why. Just know they are there. They are watching you, waiting for an opportunity to harm you in some way."

Trust no one. Never fully trust anyone but yourself. There really are people out to get me. That message was received and learned. Mom was right. Be like a duck. Rage can be in charge, but don't let anyone ever know Rage is with you.

Chapter 28

Fueled by rage and revenge, my job search kept me busy. With every department announcement of my placement on their list for hire, contempt grew. Believing I should be hired immediately, I continued to apply at every department in the county.

Three months passed since graduation, with no job offer in sight. With desperation and disgust, I began working again as a server, while awaiting news from any department.

The summer of 1996 ended as the year began: no job, no career, working as a server to support myself. Eight months went by with no interest from any department. Nine. Ten; the holidays were fast approaching. What the fuck happened to this year?

The entire year passed with nothing to show for it. Another year of my life wasted. I could see the disappointment on my mom's face every time we passed by each other. She couldn't even look at me. I looked away to avoid the intense loathing and shame I felt about myself. I could not let her see that I knew I messed up, yet again.

Mom was busier than ever with her own floral design business. She was finally living her American dream. But when she looked at me, the repugnance I felt about my life was reflected in her face. I pretended not to notice. I kept my face expressionless at all times, in and out of my room. With nothing to say to one another, we were roommates who coexisted.

Intending to make my resume more attractive to both police and fire departments, I applied to the paramedic program; classes were set to begin in January.

Sitting in the backyard, with my anatomy and physiology book, my stomach began to churn. The intensity grew faster than my breathing could contain. My whole body unleashed a primal cry, a kind of guttural cry that I could not suppress. I didn't want to suppress the feeling. The force of my tears mixed with rage, from the soles of my feet to the crown of my head; my entire body convulsed as the energy began to ooze from every pore.

After years of containing rage and disgust, I could no longer keep them in hiding. I wailed as my body excreted the toxins of shame, guilt, humiliation, and resentment. Exasperated by my inability to function in my life, I felt the energy expelling itself from my body. Exhausted by the amount of energy required to camouflage my feelings, I surrendered. In the privacy of my backyard, I sobbed. And I just let it all go until there was nothing left.

Once the energy left my body and I was able to breathe, I felt a calming sensation filling me, a warm, soothing feeling that began in the tips of my toes and worked its way to the crown of my head.

It's going to be okay. I'm going to be okay. I heard my own voice speaking to me. *Go do what you know you want to do. There is no reason to be afraid anymore.* The voice in my head spoke with conviction and clarity. I deeply needed to listen.

I got up and walked into the house with purpose. I picked up the phone with composure and dialed it.

The voice on the other end greeted me, "Palmer College of Chiropractic; how may I help you?"

"Hi, is this the admissions office?" I asked. "My name is Natacha Nelson. I was a student from 1993 to 1995. I want to know how I can re-enroll."

"Can you come in this afternoon to discuss your options?" the advisor asked.

"Yes, I can," I replied. "Thank you."

The palliative sensation ebbed through my entire body, a deep inner sense that I was making the right decision. Finally, the perfectly right decision, for me.

I walked through the hallway to the office and knew this was where I belonged. I just didn't know it until then.

Chapter 29

As the first chord of "Pomp and Circumstance" resonated from the auditorium walls, I tilted my head back so the forming tears drained in the back of my throat instead of rolling down my cheeks. With each step toward my seat, I saw flashes of my failing college grades, letters of dismissal from Santa Clara University and the police department, driving three and four times weekly to Stanford University for treatment. I made it. I was graduating. I found a way to climb out of the pit of failure I fell into. I searched for Mom in the crowd; she was sitting next to my cousins; we smiled as our eyes met. Both of us were keenly aware of the curved, crooked path my life had taken to get me there. Our smiles exchanged the love we felt for one another, which neither of us vocalized.

As the background music faded, a chorus of songs by Pearl Jam played a tribute in my mind to the past ten years of my life.

Oh, I, oh, I'm still alive.

Hey, I, oh, I'm still alive.

Yeah, yeah, yeah, yeah."

"Today is a special day." The dean's voice reverberated in the microphone. I snapped back to the auditorium, where I sat among my graduating peers, exhaling as pride filled my lungs. I relaxed in my seat for the ceremony, but a movement in the back of the room caught my attention.

His six-foot, four-inch frame glided across the room, making his way to an open seat. Unable to contain my tears, I allowed them to flow down my cheeks as I looked down at my hands folded on my lap.

My dad is here, I thought. *My dad showed up. How did he know?*

I hadn't told him about graduation. I knew Mom did not tell him about it. Seven years had gone by since I last saw or spoke to my father. Prior to that meeting, I had seen my father only once in the preceding six years.

My heart pounded with joy, sprinkled with feelings of betrayal. In that moment, none of the past mattered; I was Daddy's girl. He came there that day to see me. The little girl in me wanted the ceremony to hurry to completion so I could hug him. My dad was there to see me, to be with me, there for me.

After the ceremony, we gathered in the common area, rushing through exchanging congratulatory hugs and well wishes for the future. I said goodbye to my colleagues, knowing we would most likely not cross paths again. I wanted to get to my family.

I held my breath and hugged my dad. The little girl inside of me was acutely aware that I was now tall enough to look directly in his eyes without looking up at him. His beaming smile still lit up the room and made my heart melt. Confused by the swirling mixture of joy, rage, and resentment I felt for him right then, I hugged him again to hide the tears wanting to come out.

I said my final goodbyes to my school comrades; my family and friends had agreed on a special dinner. My fullest, loving heart extended an invitation to my dad to savor more time with him, not knowing when our next time together would be.

When he declined, I put my bravest face on to say goodbye. In the same smooth fashion that he waltzed into the auditorium, he glided out the door. My twenty-eight-year-old doctor self stood with stoic confidence. My five-year-old self wanted to reach out and grab my daddy's leg, preventing him from getting into his car.

There was a hole in my heart in the shape of my father, once again, raw. The scar tissue was never as strong as I wished it would be. The sorrow and grief of my father's absence sheared open my heart, leaving me, once again, with the work of suturing the pieces back together. I pushed the agony into the pit of my intestines, which I had become a master at. I sat with family and friends to celebrate my achievement.

Beginning Monday, I had an office to go to, with patients to care for. I was a doctor; no time to waste feeling sad about my dad. Time to be done and move on; enough already.

Chapter 30

From the moment I returned to school, a deep inner drive filled me with the desire to succeed as a chiropractor. My focus to build my practice was laser sharp; my own inner drive was now my fuel.

Although I took the scenic route through school, once graduation was done, none of the distractions of my past seemed to matter. Here I was, with a degree and an office, where working as an associate granted me the opportunity to learn the skills of a private practice.

Each day, I walked into the office with my heart filled with joy. Although my body was bursting with gratitude and pride for the challenging road I had traveled, it was time to move forward and not look back. No one needed to know of the path I took to get there; all that mattered was that I was there now. The past was past; no need to talk about the past. No need to acknowledge history. The diploma on the wall gave me permission to never look back.

In the final year of school, I connected with a local indoor volleyball facility, looking for an adult league to join. Nine years had gone by since I last played on a team, but my childlike delight for playing never ceased. For nine years, my love of playing volleyball had been stymied. Until now, that love energy had nowhere to go, nowhere to flow. Playing in a league opened me to a deeper level of wonder and appreciation. I had the same feelings I experienced in seventh grade, the first time I hit a ball. The indoor facility also had a sand court. My heart pulled me to play, and I listened.

I finally felt like I was where I belonged, doing what I was meant to be doing. There was a flow to my days, a sense of ease of growing my practice and playing volleyball. I spent every weekend at the beach playing volleyball, meeting new people; friends and patients were intertwined. I was content. Every day, for the first time, I felt content with my life.

I spent all my free time at the beach and the college campus sand courts. I couldn't get enough playing beach volleyball. I played in local tournaments and even drove to Southern California to participate in the large events. My world was expanding.

In an effort to build my practice, I brought a portable chiropractic table to the beach on the weekends, when the tournaments were taking place. I made sure to introduce myself and my work to everyone. I recognized one player in the Women's Open division from my time at the beach. She lived here and played on the professional volleyball tour. She traveled to all the tournaments and competed during the summer. I was in awe of watching her play; she and her volleyball partner played at a higher level than anyone else I had seen. I was not surprised to hear of her top professional finishes.

As I worked on her, she invited me to train with her. I practically jumped out of my skin to say yes. I was unable to contain my joy.

She complemented me on my skills and potential, and invited me to train with her regularly. I accepted her offer, which brought me to the courts six days each week. I absorbed all of her insights and knowledge, and could see my level of play drastically improve. Now my volleyball partner and I were beginning to win more matches and able to compete in the higher rated open-level events.

For the entire summer and into the off-season, I trained with her. I watched my level consistently improve; the impulse to play at a higher level began to gnaw in me, but I pushed the thought aside as a dumb idea I needed to keep secret. There was no way I could ever play at her level. I was content to play in my local events and keep my childish dreams to myself.

One day, she told me about an Association of Volleyball Professionals (AVP) event in Santa Cruz; she was playing and suggested I try to attend as a chiropractor to work on the athletes during the event. I squealed in delight when she informed me of the upcoming event.

"I'll connect you with the director," she said. As promised, she made sure that I was the chiropractor on site, in the player tent, for the event.

I set up my table in the player tent for the event and began to introduce myself to all of the players, officials, crew members, everyone associated with the AVP.

"You know," she said one day, "you are good enough to play in the AVP qualifiers now. Even if you don't make it through the rounds to get into the main draw, you can experience the levels of play and test your abilities."

"There's no way I can compete at this level," I protested.

"You may not win, but you can always compete. The next event is Hermosa Beach in June. You have nothing to lose; it's one of the largest beach events of the year."

Her words echoed in my ears: "You may not win, but you can always compete." She spoke with a powerful force. Trusting her, I made the choice to compete in the event. My volleyball partner and I agreed that regardless of the outcome, we would compete and enjoy the great event.

In June 2000, the Hermosa Beach AVP event did not disappoint. The stadium court was on a grand scale, surrounded by more courts than were set up in Santa Cruz. Combined with a two-story skate ramp, the energy on the pier was electric as we checked in for our court assignment and match time.

We stepped onto the groomed court; the pristine sand was even from corner to corner, not a single footprint. On the empty stadium court, the referee blew his whistle and waved his arm, signaling us to begin. We competed and won. It was such a high, the exhilaration of playing at a higher level; we played better than I thought we were capable of playing. It touched a place in my soul I was unaware of. Although my AVP initiation ended in the second round, the stirring of my heart awakened.

Walking on the pier after our loss, I could feel my body present, yet I was distant. I wasn't tired, just distracted, unable to choose a restaurant to eat dinner, unable to process the deep sensation coursing through my body. There was euphoria from the win and loss, from competing. But there was something else, something happening in my body, beyond understanding. A deep inner knowing radiating, reverberating up and down my spine, giving me chills.

It's time, I acknowledged to myself, afraid to say out loud what I knew to be true. In a haze, I enjoyed the remainder of the event and the weekend, keeping my secret to myself.

When I got home to my bed, I was restless, as my mind chatter would not cease.

What the fuck are you thinking? You have your whole life here. You have everything you need; everything you worked toward is here. Why are you going to screw it all up? You just got your shit together. Don't go fucking it all up now by moving to Southern California, where you have nothing, you fucking idiot.

I answered myself, *I don't need to tell anyone. I will keep my secret quiet, in case it doesn't happen, in case it doesn't work out. Al least for now, I'll just see.*

On Monday morning, I called two players I met at the AVP event in Santa Cruz, acknowledging it was a long shot but I hoped to hear back from one of them. I made peace with myself that I would drop the idea of moving if I did not hear back, sort of a sign from the God I didn't really believe in. But I had to try, just to make sure.

One of the players, Scott, called me back.

"Yeah, I know of a couple chiropractic offices here," he said. "I don't know if they are looking for an associate, but here are their numbers."

Appreciative of the follow-up lead, I left a message with the chiropractor. Again, I was unsure if I would hear back and knew it was a long shot. But I had to follow up, just for my own peace of mind.

The next day, Tuesday, I had a phone interview, which ended with a contract in the mail on Friday for my associate position to commence July. I was shock and stunned. I had not yet told the doctor I currently worked for or Mom.

I was anxious to share the news with Mom but afraid of her disappointing glare as I revealed my latest dumb idea. Yet the desire to move drew me in with such force, I was able to face her to make my announcement.

While volleyball was the catalyst that lured me away from my hometown, in my heart, I knew I needed a fresh start to my life. I knew deep inside that it was time for me to grow, expand, and find more of me than I could find in San Jose.

Besides, I thought, *it's probably only going to be for a few years anyway. By then, I will probably want a family and will need to move back for that.* I convinced myself I was doing the right thing. I packed my car with as many necessities as I could squeeze in, put Journey's *Greatest Hits* in the CD player, and turned up the volume to muffle my cries as I watched Mom's figure appear smaller and smaller in my rearview mirror. The five o'clock dawning light came up just behind her face, illuminating her smile and waving hand.

PART 3

Chapter 31

Sitting in my private office, upstairs from the treating room, I heard the humming of voices downstairs as staff and patients greeted one another. I reviewed the day's patient files; it was a full day. It'd been just two years since relocating to the Los Angeles area. I had the pleasure of treating patients every day; I knew I was really good at my work. I loved being a chiropractor. Operating a day-to-day business was challenging. I learned managing, marketing, and all of the work that went on behind the scenes of owning and operating a business, I was not aware of how much time and energy was required. But I was learning and figuring out how to make it work.

I included time for volleyball. Now I had a coach I worked with weekly and set up training with other people, including weekends, keeping my toes in the sand six days a week. The plethora of players and sunshine gave me constant access to play.

I didn't regret leaving San Jose. My life here was a dream, better than I thought. I was happy I listened to the little voice that encouraged me to move,. Although moving felt right, I was uncomfortable leaving the safety and security of my hometown. I especially liked that no one knew my past; no one knew my secrets and my failures. No one need ever find out, since my past no longer existed here. The past could not touch me.

"Dr. Nelson," my receptionist said through the intercom, "your mom is on line 1."

I was jolted back to my desk. *That's weird*, I thought. *Mom never calls me on work mornings. It's 6:45; something must be wrong. I shouldn't answer it; I don't want to hear any bad news.*

"Hi, Mom, what's going on," I finally said, picking up. "Everything okay?"

"Your father is in the hospital," she replied. "He collapsed last night but is stable now. You may want to come up to see him, I am not sure of the situation."

"Okay, Mom," I said, stunned. "I'll be there tomorrow."

Closing my eyes, I reveled in my dad's hug from graduation and the lure of his magnetic smile when he walked into the auditorium.

"Dr. Nelson," my receptionist said, as the crackling intercom shook me back to the present. "The treatment rooms are full, and the waiting room is overflowing."

I could not think about my dad now. There was no time for tears or to feel scared about what was happening. I would be there tomorrow. For now, I needed to work, to put my smile on, the one patients grew to appreciate, the one they wanted to see from me. Patients didn't want a sad doctor; they were here for me to support them, to be here for them. My job was to take care of them first. I couldn't let anyone know something was wrong; I wouldn't let anyone see that I was upset.

The weight of my body pinned me to my seat. Silence filled my head for the one-hour flight to Oakland. I refused to allow any negative thoughts about Dad's condition to enter my mind. Gratefully, Mom was silent as she drove me to the hospital. My mind raced to prepare myself for what I might see, what I might hear. I could not let my little girl self have a meltdown; she needed to be strong.

When did my six-foot, four-inch dad become so tiny? I thought when I entered his room.

The frame of the man beneath the hospital sheets looked so frail; this could not be his body. His scrawny legs were no bigger than the width of my calf. His big, dancing brown eyes were dull and lifeless. This was not my father; this could not be Darnel, the vivacious, high-spirited man I knew. When did he become so fragile? Graduation was less than four years ago; what happened?

"It's good to see you, kiddo," he whispered.

I sat on the edge of his bed, biting my lower lip to make it stop quivering, hoping the pain would stop my tears.

"Hi, Dad." My shaking voice betrayed me. I hugged him, which confirmed that this frail and fragile man under the blanket was indeed my dad. My little girl self began to shake as the significance of what I was seeing confronted my soul.

I hugged him as though twenty years of unspoken conversations could be expressed in one moment.

Maybe if I squeezed him hard enough, long enough, I can coerce him to say what I want to hear, I thought. *Maybe if I squeeze him a little harder, he'll feel compelled to answer the questions in my head: Why did you leave me, Dad? Why did you hurt us so much? Why did you ...?*

"It's good to see you, too, Dad," was all I could say; the moment was gone. The answers to those questions would remain his secrets. I suspected I'd never get to know.

As I looked at my dad's face, the previously unseen gray hairs were obvious to me now. The opaque fog in his left eye made him turn his head slightly to look at me. Our eyes met, sharing a connection for a split-second. His gaze drifted to a distant place behind me.

Mom had been sitting quietly in the guest chair in the far corner, but the twenty-five years of unspoken secrets between them were present in the room. The heavy discomfort of their relationship history forced me to get up to catch the passing doctor in the hall.

The doctor stopped to explain Dad's prognosis:

"Your father collapsed and is suffering the effects of long-term alcohol poisoning. Sunday night, he passed out and hit his head. Luckily, someone heard him fall and called the medics. His liver and kidneys are very weak. If your father continues to drink, he will die soon."

My rage monster was emerging in full force. This was all due to his drinking. Alcohol poisoning? Are you fucking kidding me? How much was he drinking now? What the fuck? He knew he had a problem; his wife knew he had a problem. Her three gown boys should know he has a problem. Why wasn't anyone helping him? Why was his family ignoring his disease, helping him to get sober? What was wrong with them? Was I the only one who wanted to help him? I couldn't bring him to LA. Maybe I could find a way to pay for a facility for him here. I didn't know how I would do that; my office barely broke even each month with the school and business loan payments.

Maybe I needed to move back to Northern California to be closer to him and take care of him? I was his daughter and could see he was dying; no one else seemed to care. I didn't know how to help him. I didn't know what to do. I lived so far away, I felt helpless. It was excruciating to watch him withering, dying a slow death. Being a doctor and not being able to help my dad was demoralizing.

Visiting hours inched their way to the end. I didn't want to go, didn't want to say goodbye. I didn't want our story to end like this. Intense pain gripped my heart, as I collapsed on Dad to hug him; I feared this would be the last time I'd see him alive.

"I love you, kiddo," he whispered in my ear, his words giving me permission to cry.

His hospital gown drenched in my tears, I finally found the courage to pull away. I walked to the door; bracing myself, I turned to look at him.

"I love you, too, Dad."

It took the distance from the hospital room to Mom's car to gather my composure. Mom never liked to see me cry, for any reason. She didn't like to see me upset; I needed to put my sad face away before I got to the car.

The little girl with a broken heart sat silently in her mom's car. I knew not to talk about my father with her. She remained neutral, nothing to say, good or bad. Jut silence. I followed her lead.

With so many conflicting emotions, I returned to work the following day. Not knowing what to do with the pain in my heart, I did the one thing I knew, with absolute certainly, would comfort me: I went to work.

Taking care of patients and diving into the day-to-day business, which I now knew how to do, separated me from my father's condition. At work, I was really good at what I did: caring for patients. I felt helpful taking care of their needs; I felt useful. In my office, I was the doctor with answers, the doctor who had advice and was able to console her patients.

In my office, I could put my focus and energy on the patients. I allowed the business to consume me. My uncomfortable feelings didn't exist while in my office. They didn't exist on the volleyball court, either. As long as I was spending all my waking hours in one or the other, I could keep my promise to myself and not need to feel anything. The office was my constant guarantee that there was always work to do, work for me to get lost in.

I heard from my cousins that my father was home with his wife; he was doing fine. He was enjoying retirement with his sons. My dad certainly knew how to land on his feet. He was okay, back to his life. I continued to live mine: a busy private practice, training and competing in the top volleyball events, and living with a kind and gentle man who had fallen in love with me.

I, too, was fine. Really, I was just fine.

Chapter 32

On Tuesday, April 29, 2003, the phone rang.

"Hi, kiddo," he said. "Just calling to say hi." The familiar and unmistakable slur of alcohol reverberated through the phone. Ugh, it was 7 a.m.

"Hi, Dad," I said, cutting our conversation short. "I have to go. I'm on my way to work. You good?"

"Yeah, I'm good. Just wanted to hear your voice. Love you, kiddo."

"Love you, too, Dad."

This was the first time hearing my dad's voice since the hospital incident. The sound of alcohol on his voice made me cringe; I was unable, unwilling to engage in any conversation with him. Maybe over the weekend, I could catch him sober. If not, maybe sometime soon.

On Friday, May 2, my receptionist rang through the intercom.

"Dr. Nelson, your mom is on line 1."

"Hey, Mom, what's up?" I asked.

"I'm calling to tell you your dad was found dead this morning," she replied. "His wife just called me to tell you. She will let us know of the funeral arrangements. I'm sorry, baby."

'What do you mean, he is dead?" I cried. "This can't be true; he just called me three days ago."

I suddenly realized the call on Tuesday was his birthday, and I didn't even acknowledge it. I just rushed him off the phone, not wanting to engage with him. I was hurt and disappointed, angry at him. Honestly, I was always angry at him. A part of me even hated him.

I had been waiting for this call for the past year. Believing this call would arrive soon, I felt myself prepared, but not then. I was not ready for it then. I felt caught off guard, unprepared. I let myself believe he was fine, hearing from relatives that his health was stable. Dad was a big strong man; he was supposed to figure his way out of this. Darnel always figured a way out; he was smart, a survivor.

I wondered how to tell my little girl self to get through this. What was I supposed to say? I didn't know. The little girl who just lost her daddy was lost. But this big girl doctor needed to get her shit together and get downstairs to work. There were rooms of patients and a full waiting room. They all needed her help.

Sorry, little girl, I said to myself. *No time for you; I can't deal with you right now. I have to take care of business. Stay strong. Suck it up. It doesn't matter; he hasn't been a part of our lives for twenty years. None of it matters now. Dad is gone. Put on your best, most believable brave face; we have people to take care of, people who need us, people who are here to see us, who want us to take care of them. Besides, there is too much riding on this business; I carry a lot of responsibilities and owe a lot in loans. Dad cannot interfere with our ability to take care of us. We don't have the time to think about him or grieve for him. Not now; maybe someday.*

Chapter 33

I made my way onto the plane. It'd been one week since receiving the news of my father's death. Although I worked all week, I felt off. I hoped the patients didn't notice;1 I did my best 1to keep my personal news private; they didn't need to know. I could 1not let my father interfere with my work.

At the airport, my mother's expression flat. No sadness, no grief, no joy. Just detached. At least Mom was consistent in her response to anything related to my father.

We were early to the funeral home. I went in on my own; Mom offered me space to be alone before the service. I walked through the door; no one was inside. Looking to my right, I saw his casket. It was open. My breath stopped. I didn't know this was going to be an open-casket service.

I slowly made my way toward him, the American flag beside the casket reminding me of his service in the army, which I knew of and yet know nothing about.

Hi, kiddo. You made it, I heard. His voice was clear. No slurring, no remnants of alcohol. His voice in my head was smiling, just the way I always wished.

Staring at his face, I gripped the casket rail to prop me up. Years of withheld tears surged to the surface with an uncontrollable force, and with a single wail, I crumpled to the floor, sobbing.

I was sobbing for the little girl who would never get to know her father, for the little girl who would never see her daddy again, for the little girl who didn't know her father, her sober father, her real father. I was the little girl with a gigantic hole in her heart that she didn't know how to fill, the little girl who never felt like daddy's little girl.

Grief, despair, regret, and sadness came rushing out of every pore. The silent screams from every cell released their acidic content that had been trapped for decades, reverberating through my body. Anger and loathing penetrated through my eyes looking at my father's corpse, looking completely at peace. This little girl was inconsolable. Not wanting to engage with family or guests, I sat in the front row, burying my face in tissue.

I couldn't look at my relatives. I didn't want them to know. I didn't want them to know I hadn't spoken to my father this entire year since my hospital visit, that I had hung up on him when he called the morning of his birthday. I didn't want them to know that I could have found a way to pay for treatment, so he could get sober. But most of all, I didn't want anyone to know the shame I felt, that in my heart, I had discarded him as my father. I gave up on him. I no longer wanted him to be my father.

As his casket closed, I buried daddy's little girl with him. I could not take her back to LA with me. She was in too much pain. She was hurting too much. And she would get me in trouble if I didn't get rid of her. I could not let her exist any longer; she was too emotional, too vulnerable, too weak, too much of a liability.

Back at work Monday morning, fun, quirky, silly Dr. Nelson was replaced by serious, somber Dr. Nelson. This new version of doctor Nelson smiled, did her job exceedingly well, and was highly efficient. No longer feeling playful or joyful, I doubled down on my efforts to build a larger practice and focus on my future. New Dr. Nelson was engaging but never got personal. She was incredibly caring and proficient at caring for patients' needs, even before they knew they needed help. Delightful Dr. Nelson had been replaced with punctual, purposeful, functional Dr. Nelson. No one seemed to mind; no one seemed to care. No one noticed. And that was fine with me.

Chapter 34

I was consumed by my practice and the business. Every waking moment, when not playing volleyball, my focus was on growing the practice. I poured my energy, time, money, and resources into the business, with the sole intention to grow my practice to maximum capacity.

I was close to achieving my goal. In fact, spending that time on the beach playing volleyball no longer fulfilled me.

I had been in LA for seven years. While I had the opportunity to compete in tournaments around the world, I was not having the success I wanted with my rankings. Knowing I was not able to dedicate myself full time to train, it was time to let go of volleyball and direct all of my energy to growing the practice.

I spent fourteen, sometimes sixteen hours a day focusing on patients and marketing; it was paying off. The extra work taking part in community speaking engagements, having booths at local fairs, and making phone calls and emails all began to show dividends.

On a clear blue Monday, I went into the office early to prepare. Summer was rapidly approaching. A seemingly ordinary day, nothing out of character scheduled. A pleasant effervescent energy filled the office. I felt it, the staff felt it, even the patients felt it. But no one could articulate what it was. The energy was intense, focused, fun, light, and highly charged; there was a spring in our step as we moved about the day, just a notch below controlled chaos.

After the last patient of the day left, having given every ounce of energy to the order of the day, I crumpled on a chair next to my staff.

"Wow, what a day," I said. "It seemed full, nonstop, the entire day."

"It was," the receptionist said, amazed. "Today, every patient who was scheduled to come in, showed up. We even had some walk-ins. Every available time slot was taken; the entire day, not a single person missed or rescheduled."

"Holy shit," I replied. "I did it. We did it. We experienced a one-of-a-kind day, a maximum-capacity day. By practice management standards, it was a perfect day."

The decision to pour all of myself into the practice had been the right choice.

As I lay in bed, the electric charge of the day's success coursed through my body. Success; this was what success felt like. I knew I should feel elated, but I didn't. I knew I provided wonderful service. I knew I helped many people feel better and should feel content with my work.

I didn't feel sad. I didn't feel content. I felt empty. Achieving my perfect day just didn't feel the way I thought I would. Checking off the box on my "goals and to-do" list made my face smile but not my heart.

Ten days passed. My perfect-day hangover continued to linger. While I loved my daily exchanges with people, the day-to-day grind took a toll. I felt empty. The pace I was living at was unsustainable. My head simultaneously knew this was true and found it difficult to relinquish control. I feared that if I slowed down, I would lose everything I had worked so hard for. I gave myself permission to back off the marketing and enjoy the fruits of my efforts. I thought I could refill my energy tank; it sounded ideal but unrealistic. I knew I should, I probably could, I just didn't feel like I could.

Emptiness surged and morphed into sadness. The bullish stride I pursued my business endeavors with now paused; I focused on all other aspects of life. I had been married three years now; the rumbling of wanting more made its presence known.

I want a family, my heart whispered.

Chapter 35

Sitting on the edge of the bathtub, my period once again showed up. I knew becoming pregnant could take years, but I couldn't shake the feeling that I may not be able to conceive a child of my own.

Maybe the amount of stress and damage I subjected my body to from binging and purging was beginning to show the consequences. Maybe when I was twenty-six and my OB/GYN found a tumor in my right ovary, it was a sign I was not going to become a mother.

At the time, I was too naive to believe the doctor's words, which now haunted me:

"The tumor on your ovary is the size of a grapefruit. I will surgically remove the tumor and the ovary, and look at the other one. If there's any sign of tumorous growth, I'll remove that one too, as a precaution."

At twenty-six, I was not ready for a family, but I begged the doctor to leave my good ovary, regardless of how it looked. Alone and innocent, I proceeded with the surgeon, hoping he would listen to my pleas. After surgery, the doctor announced he left my good ovary in, seeing no signs of trauma or damage. Since my menstrual cycle had been normal and timely each month, I never considered the possibility of not having a child. I dreamed of my little girl since Olivia showed up on *The Cosby Show*.

At first sight, I knew I was supposed to be a mother to a little girl. Olivia made her debut on *The Cosby Show* in 1988. Never before had I seen a mixed-race child on television, or anywhere in the media. She was the first little girl I saw on television or movies who looked like me. She was welcomed, featured, and loved on the show and in the magazines that wrote about her. Her face was seared in my heart; she was my inner warrior who battled against the people who told me growing up that "girls like me aren't allowed to be mommies."

Chapter 36

Running the practice, a marriage, and being unable to conceive took its toll. Feeling strangled by life, desperate for a break, I told my husband I wanted to see my family for Christmas, alone. I drove home for the holidays, crying the 350 miles to San Jose, which now felt more like home than LA. Maybe it was time to move back. Maybe I was unable to become pregnant because all my family and support was in the Bay Area. Maybe I just need some good home cooking, from both Mom and my cousin. My soul needed nourishment.

I knew Mom could see the anguish on my face. I was grateful she didn't prod me about my solo travels. I didn't want to worry her. I didn't want her to know that she may never be a grandmother; she had been asking, hoping, nudging since the wedding. I had no answers for her. I silently avoided mentioning the pink elephant in the room.

Nourished, I drove back to LA, realizing more than two years had passed by since I last played volleyball. I missed playing. I missed the energy of meeting with friends for a morning of friendly competition. I missed the social camaraderie, the laughter, the silliness of playing to offset the seriousness of work and life. Excited at reconnecting with friends, I set up games for that weekend.

I knew I had not played in over two years, but I had been working out, although I could not tell based on how lethargic and heavy I felt trying to move and jump in the sand. My skills were rusty, and I played like a novice attending an adult community beach class.

At least I loved the girls I was with. They didn't care that I was not playing up to par; we set up games midweek, our "Welcome to the New Year" celebration.

The office mail piled up in my absence; one day, there was a package that looked more appealing than any letter.

It was a box from my childhood friend, Amanda. It'd been years since our last visit. Living in different states, we did our best to connect through handwritten letters, our communication choice since Duran Duran brought us together in summer camp, circa 1985.

She sent homemade chocolate chip cookies and a handmade baby blanket. I never shared with her we were trying; I suspected she was sending me hinting nudges as well, having her own young daughter. Her note wished me well and hoped I enjoyed motherhood sometime in the future. Not wanting to face the possibility of my little Olivia not becoming reality, I stashed the blanket in the supply closet. I made a mental note to thank her later, after the emotional swell calmed.

Day two of volleyball; still sucking at this game. My lungs felt like I was inhaling shards of glass; I was jumping no higher than a credit card, and my legs felt like bricks were tied to them. My game was really off; if I want to play in a local tournament this summer, I had a lot of work to do. I really missed playing, though. I looked forward to the training and the challenge of coming back.

Day three, back on the sand. *At some point*, I thought, *this has to feel easier, even a little. Fuck, I feel old.* Why was getting back into volleyball shape so damn hard? I felt really run down and wondered if I had the flu; so many people around me had been sick. It'd been decades since I had the flu; I forgot what it felt like. This sucked.

On day four, I called to cancel, saying, "Sorry, guys, I need to cancel our games today. I have the flu. I've been up all night, nauseous. Not throwing up, but I feel really exhausted. I don't have much of a fever, but I don't want to get any of you girls sick."

I made my way into the kitchen; my desire for coffee had not weaned. Maybe it was the need for caffeine I was addicted to.

The taste of coffee was noticeably different this morning. The foul, rancid flavor made me spit out the first sip. Even bad coffee never tasted that bad.

I went to my doctor's office, less than a mile from home, without calling for an appointment. I knew she would see me as a walk-in. She had me pee on a stick and then wait for the results. A few minutes later, she came in with a smile on her face.

"Yep," she said. "You are pregnant."

I couldn't wait for my husband, Dan, to come home; I thought of the gift box and called Amanda. "How did you know?" I asked. "I didn't even know."

"I had a dream that you were pregnant," she replied, "and when I awoke, God told me to send you the blanket, so I did."

I burst into tears, relieved, as the fear fled my body. Comfort soothed my heart, and I shared the news with Mom on the phone.

When Dan got home, he smiled at the news and wrapped his arms around me. Exalted, I fell asleep on our oversized sofa chair. My little Olivia was on her way.

I stopped drinking coffee, and as the caffeine withdrawal headache surged, my four cups per day grabbed my attention. I tried to lay on the couch and nap, unsuccessfully, acutely aware of the distance and disconnection between me and my body. To be pregnant and not know, to not feel it. The intense, violent, vigorous pulsing in my head was an urgent reminder of how abandoned I had become to myself.

When did I become so estranged to myself? I promised never to cease this connection, to myself, to my body, to this miracle growing inside of me. I thanked, God, though I was still not sure I believed in him.

Chapter 37

Pregnancy rekindled a sense of appreciation, love, and awe for my body, for the human body. It was the same reverence I discovered in chiropractic school. Reading through my women's health and pregnancy books, I was brought back to my first set of Time-Life hardcover books. The specific edition had the front cover with a picture of a man's hand and a child's hand laying over it. At five years old, I fell in love with the picture series of a baby from conception to birth. I stared at them for hours. In that moment, at age five, I knew I wanted to be a doctor.

Right now, my most important patients were me and my baby.

Feeling a deep connection with my baby, momma bear rising, her defiant warrior self grew more intense and more fierce each day. The choice to have a midwife and deliver our child at home felt normal and natural and the best for us. The fear of labor pain did not deter me. I had a deep respect and understanding for the human body; gestation and delivery were a part of the process. It was an experience I wanted to be fully present for and connected with. We made preparations with our midwife.

I flipped the calendar: October. My baby would be arriving this month. Thought the doctor said the fifth; that date seemed arbitrary and unscientific to me. My baby should arrive on its own schedule. We opted to not learn the baby's gender after the ultrasound. One of nature's ultimate surprises, we wanted him/her to make his/her presence known, beginning with the announcement on arrival day.

October fifth came and went. Maybe on my birthday I'd be graced with this precious gift. Nope, this little one let me know we would not be sharing a birthday. Three weeks past due date, I was not worried but growing weary as my seventy-five-pound weight gain, in addition to my large belly, had made day-to-day functions difficult.

During my final check-in with the backup medical doctor, he let me know he was not in agreement with my beliefs; he declared that if this baby did not come out on its own by October 20, I needed to check into the hospital for induction.

I spoke with my unborn child, letting it know of my desire to have a safe delivery in the comfort of our home, surrounded by its father, my mother, and the midwife, who had been present and caring for us since the beginning. *However, I conceded to my belly, if my plan is not in okay for you, I will go to the hospital.*

I could not bring myself to pack an overnight hospital bag before crawling into bed Monday October 20. At 2:30 a.m., the unmistakable, intense stabbing pain of the first contraction made me scream. Pained but relieved, Dan called the midwife.

The guttural, primal screams from our bedroom, I suspect, arose the suspicions of the neighbors, ready to call the police.

At 9:46 a.m., my little Olivia graced us with her presence. My daughter Jasmine was born, sharing the same birthday as my friend Amanda's daughter.

Chapter 38

The action steps of mothering didn't feel particularly difficult; changing diapers, nursing, and so on were just part of the growing list of things to do. What I was not prepared for was the amount of emotional energy motherhood required.

This little bundle of scrumptious, yummy joy was making my heart expand, and love just oozed out. My expanding heart was increasingly aware of the immense responsibility of keeping Jasmine safe. My heart opening was uncomfortable. I could no longer function with the laser sharp acuity I prided myself on for success. The financial responsibility, riddled with accompanying fears of not being able to provide for her, kept me awake most nights.

I wanted to stay home with my baby. I wanted to be with her, snuggle her, and nap with her. I wanted to do right by her. The business had been showing signs of decline since I stopped adjusting patients six months ago. I stepped aside for another doctor to work with patients while taking on the role as office manager to maintain connection with business operations, but it was an ill fit for me.

I felt as though I lost control of the office; the signs of the business declining had been visible for months. I just didn't want to acknowledge them, at least not yet. Not then; I wanted to savor my pregnancy and for a short time just not care about the business or working out or maintaining any sense of control. Once the baby arrived, I'd feel more inclined to be on a schedule again. I'd feel the desire to work again. For then, I just pretended I didn't see my practice dwindling in front of me. I pretended I couldn't see the truth because I didn't want to be in charge. I couldn't do what was required of me as the doctor, and I didn't want to. I ignored the symptoms that the business was failing and focused on my health. I couldn't do both. I couldn't allow my body to feel the stress. I just pretended all was fine for now.

I needed to go back to work to salvage what I could. Jasmine was one week old; my body felt beat up, but I could not allow my practice to disintegrate. It was our only source of income.

I had to go back to work; my body didn't feel strong, my mind didn't feel stable, but this was what I had to do. My heart was torn. Anger overpowered the joy and love that my heart was simmering in. The fear of losing my practice, the business I poured my heart into, was too much for me to consider as a real possibility. I could no longer watch and do nothing. I didn't want to care for anyone else right now. I didn't want to be responsible for anyone's health right now. I just wanted to take care of my baby, my body, my health. I only had enough energy for us, and I didn't want to have to give away any of it to anyone else. But I had to.

Rancid anger festered every day I went to work, unable to be home with my baby. Discontent brewed; neither Dan nor I was happy in this marriage. There were loud, unmistakable silences that neither of us wanted to acknowledge. I brought Jasmine to work, in part to not be home where the energy of a lackluster marriage lingered.

There was no time for pity, no time for wishing life was different. This was the way my life was; I created this. I needed to suck it up and deal with it. Pick my head up, shut up, and get to work. Focus on the business and my baby.

On Jasmine's second Christmas, Mom opted to come to LA to celebrate with us. Friends were hosting a New Year's party; it was our chance to get out and socialize. Before enjoying the holiday cheer, the secret I held was bursting at the seams, threatening to explode if I didn't speak up.

I invited Mom for a walk; the three of us went on a leisurely stroll. The anxiety of the news I wanted to share made breathing difficult. I was scared to tell her.

"Mom, I want to leave my marriage." I bit my lip as I spoke, my voice was barely audible, but she heard me and turned on me in a flash.

"No, no, no," she cried. "I didn't raise you this way. I stood there on your wedding day when you said your vows. You made a commitment to God that you need to keep. You have a child now; how can you be so selfish?"

Walking back alone with the stroller, I thought, *She's right. How can I be so selfish? We have a child now. I'm not allowed to do this to her, to us, just because I'm unhappy. That's unacceptable. Why did you even tell her? You knew she wasn't going to approve. She's right; my feelings don't matter. Especially now, as a mother. I don't have the right to have feelings or act on them. What I want no longer matters.*

For the week of her visit, I saw it. I felt it. The way she looked at me, or rather the way she avoided looking at me. The way she left the room when I entered. My mother, who once wanted to protect me and care for me above all, was now ashamed of me, disappointed in me, in who I had become, in who I was. She was disgusted by who I had become. I didn't blame her; I didn't disagree with her. I was no longer the daughter she was proud to boast about.

Watching Mom and Jasmine hug, I was envious. I desperately longed for Mom to hug me like that, to tell me she supported me, loved me. I said nothing when we arrived at the airport. Stoic as we parted, I pulled into the grocery store parking lot and cried. I shouldn't have said anything. I should have kept my mouth shut. I cannot go through a divorce, not without Mom's support. I fucked up, again.

Chapter 39

My beautiful baby, my little girl, was walking, talking, and familiarizing herself with her big new world. She was almost two years old. Where did her baby years go? They were a blur; I missed them. I didn't really get to be with her very much. All of my big dreams, my big plans of being with her were so far removed from the reality of working so hard to keep the practice afloat. The day-to-day grind to just pay rent, a mortgage, and life's expenses; the burden weighed heavily.

Dan found work that took him on the road, away from home, in five- and six-week increments. This offers relief from the cumbersome relationship we agreed to maintain. Coupled with his work and her longing to be a grandmother, Mom offered to move to LA to be more involved with Jasmine.

Dan's work forced me into the role of full-time mother and doctor. I quickly created a working structure that accommodated the life of a single working mother. I found a way to make it work. I found myself happier when he was away than when he was home for the week in between.

Guilty feelings made their way to the surface. I felt guilty that I was happier when he was away than when he was home; what an awful wife I've become. I felt guilty for asking Mom to help with Jasmine so I could work out, which mostly consisted of playing volleyball while they watched.

I felt ashamed that I did not dedicate as many hours for the office as I had in the past; my income was drastically declining. Most months, I was unable to sustain my basic costs of living. I felt guilty that when I was home, I was too tired to do more with Jasmine than eat, watch television, and go to bed. What a bad mother; I didn't have the energy to read with her or play with her more. I felt ashamed for relying on Mom and preschool to be surrogate parents to make up for my deficiencies as a mother. I adored my daughter; I just didn't know how to be a good mother.

One night, I cried as I held Jasmine tightly in my arms; as we lay in bed, I vowed to her, "If you ever find yourself in this situation, I promise I will support you in any decision you make. I hope you never find yourself in an unhappy marriage, feeling completely alone. Whatever life brings you, whatever mistakes you make, I promise I will not turn my back on you. I will never desert you or betray you. I promise I will not force you to figure life out alone. No matter what messes you create or find yourself in, even if I don't know how to help you, I will love you. I'm sorry. I'm so sorry, baby, but I have to do this."

The promises I made to Jasmine were the vows I needed to hear. The little girl in me needed permission to move forward. She needed to know she'd still be loved, no matter what, no matter how badly she screwed up.

"Mom," I finally said, "you no longer need to help me with Jasmine if you don't want to. I am moving forward with the divorce."

My steady voice masked the shaking of my hands. I turned my face away, not wanting to see her disapproving reaction. There was no need to engage with her; my decision was final. Whether she wanted to support me or not, I had a plan; I was prepared for her choice to no longer be involved.

Dan was a kind man, a gentle man. We were such different people, with completely different ways of being. We didn't fight;

we didn't yell. We just didn't really enjoy the same things; we didn't enjoy spending time together. Both of us were unhappy. Our daughter deserved two happy parents, even if this meant her parents lived in separate homes, unmarried.

Chapter 40

Dan left. All his belongings were removed from the shelves and closets. The urge to clean and reorganize consumed me. For three days and nights, I compulsively emptied every drawer, every cupboard, and every cabinet; I discarded everything I no longer needed or wanted. I hoped removing all unnecessary items from my home would help me feel less guilty about our divorce. My broken heart needed comforting, as all my dreams of marriage and family were discarded with each item. Anxiety grew in the spaces created by the emptied house.

I hoped I was doing the right thing. I didn't know. I didn't know if I was going to be able to do this. I was so afraid of life as a single mother. Mom hadn't said anything about helping me, although she was still helping with Jasmine. I hoped I made the right choice. Right then, I felt like I made the right choice for my heart but the wrong choice for my head. I didn't know which one was right, but for then, I had to listen to my heart. I followed my head when I accepted Dan's proposal. I followed my head at our wedding. I wasn't so sure my head knew what direction was best.

A month later, the building lease for my business ended. It was a chance to downsize and simplify my office. I moved into a smaller space; the new office was smaller than any office space I occupied. It was just the right size for me to manage on my own. My new office was about one-quarter the size of the old one. I needed to sell

80 percent of the furniture and equipment to fit; the overwhelming sense of shame began to resurface. I was discouraged, demoralized, and dominated.

Financial distress consumed me. I knew this was the right move in order to salvage any semblance of my business. With the impact of the new health care laws in effect, coupled with not having the resources to work as I first did to grow my business, I was unable to recapture my former glory as a doctor. Another dream I needed to let die. The pressure, feeling rundown and broken-hearted, the financial instability churned my intestines, leaving me unable to sleep or eat. With just enough energy to feed and bathe my toddler, I fell asleep with Jasmine in my arms, worrying, *I don't think I'm going to make it.*

The intense pressure of feeling alone in caring for my child, of providing for us, was at times too much. We live month to month, uncomfortably close to the edge. Day to day, I did my best to care for my patients, grateful for the slower pace of my private office space, where I was free to cry without Jasmine seeing me. She was too young to intellectually understand, but energetically, she could feel the sadness in my heart. I was unable to be fully present with her, as my heart ached for the string of recent disappointments. I gave my promise to her, to myself, to make it up to us one day.

With my counterfeit smile, I attended business networking events, in hopes that the motto "Fake it till you make it" held merit, as it once did for me. A part of me was relieved to be in a group of professionals; we were all in a similar situation, looking to grow our business. I looked forward to the weekly meetings. I didn't feel so alone.

Once again, volleyball was my savior, coming to the rescue. Needing to feel my toes in the sand, the promise of feeling anything other than despair, I committed to playing every day. The beach was my only place of solace and respite from life's happenings. It was the only place I seemed to smile and laugh. The beach was the only place I could feel possibilities.

I had been in LA ten years. Right before I got married, I lived at the beach. Why did I give that up? Oh yeah, because I was doing what I thought was right; Dan didn't want to live in the chaos of the beach. Well, I liked the chaos of the beach life. I accepted the alcohol-induced craziness for a few months in the summer in exchange for the quietness of the remaining nine months. I would love to move closer to the beach, a little apartment just the right size for Jasmine and me. Of course, it would need a garage; parking at the beach sucked. I needed a place that was isolated enough for her to feel free to jump up and down and not have any neighbors below us or next to us. What a lovely place I painted in my mind. If only that kind of place existed and was in my budget. If only …

As I made my way to the same courts where we always played, on the same part of the beach, at the end of the same walkway where I've been playing for the past five or six years, I saw her. I didn't know who she was; I'd never seen her on this street. I walked up to her and noticed the sign she was hammering onto the building: "For Rent." Curious, I asked if I could see inside. I'd like to have a mental visual for a someday vision board.

"How much is it?" I asked

It was reasonable, exactly what I believed we could afford. Maybe someday, I'd find a place just like this.

As soon as one foot touched the sand, the lure pulled me back.

"I'll take it," I said to the property manager. "When is it available?"

"Now," she replied, dangling the keys and a rental application.

My new apartment was the new sense of hope I needed. It was an inkling of life. Somewhere, from deep within, I felt myself trying to emerge from the weight of the broken pieces of my life. Some part of me was yearning to come out, to lure me back to life. I felt it. I didn't know what it was, but I felt a thin, barely perceptible energy thread of life. It was all I needed to keep me moving forward, to feel I made the right choice, that I was going to be okay, that we were going to be okay.

The scarcity of my new apartment's decor was a perfect reflection of the energy in my heart. The empty space resonated with my soul's yearning for cleansing. The change was exactly what my heart needed. In the dawn hours, I could hear the ocean waves rolling.

I was going to be okay. I was going to get through this. My heart could finally begin to heal. This was a fresh start, a new beginning. Getting dressed for my morning networking meeting, I was inspired to hold my chin up and start over. My entire world needed to be in the care and protection of my child and me. My entire focus needed to be to ensure we were safe and provided for. Nothing else mattered now. With my mom's assistance to dedicate more time to my business, I got to work. It didn't matter if I was happy in my work; it was what I knew how to do. The option of another career was not available. It didn't matter if I liked marketing or not; I had to do it. It didn't matter if I wanted to take better care of myself than my patients; this was what I had to do now. Our survival was solely my responsibility no time to entertain any feelings in my heart.

PART 4

Chapter 41

A new apartment: I loved it. My new office was just the right size for simplicity and easy to manage. My life was starting over, a fresh clean start. But life felt the same; I felt the same. Not bad, just not interesting. I should feel happier than this; I should feel at least content, but I didn't. I couldn't quite figure out what the discontent was. I was not sad, or mad, just flat. Not excited or inspired. I felt nothing.

My energy toward the office was more of necessity than desire. I gave patients and the business the best I had to give, and yet I knew, my best was just a fraction of what I gave in the past. I was fatigued and emotionally depleted. I felt empty every day. What I offered my patients was so little compared to my former self. What I had to give as a mother, I felt guilty for not being able to do more and be more for her. Jasmine deserved more than what I had to give.

"Hi, Harpreete," I said to my friend. "Come on in. How's school going? What book are you reading now?"

Harpreete's radiant smile and hug always made me feel appreciated. She showed me her book: *Loyalty to Your Soul*.

The title intrigued me. I reached for the book; the front cover flashed to my networking group. This was the same book the psychologist had with her the past few meetings, although I didn't ask; my curiosity was piqued.

"This is the second time I've seen this book," I said. "I need to go get it."

"Here, you can borrow mine," she said. "I don't need it right now."

This may help me get out of this funk, I thought. *I know I need something, I just don't know what.*

"When are you done with school?" I asked.

"I graduate in six months. Completing this master's program, with work and a new baby, feels challenging, but I'm so glad I am doing this."

"You sound happy," I said, "and you look great. Keep up the great work. Thanks for the book; we can compare notes next time."

I loved reading, now more than ever. I loved books, especially the psychology/self-help genre. I knew books had saved me and were my constant companion in my best and lowest times in my life. I could always find refuge and a spark back to life in a good book. *Loyalty to Your Soul* was just the right book for me. Seeing it twice within a month didn't seem like a coincidence now.

"Thank you for this book, Harpreete," I said when we next met. "It was just what I needed."

"You're welcome," she said. "The authors are instructors at my school. It's part of my curriculum. Are you doing okay?"

"Just stuff on my mind about my ex-husband and Jasmine I am dealing with. I wish your teachers could tell me what to do."

"I know it's short notice," she replied, "but there's an open house tonight. I can go with you, if you want. Hearing them speak always helps, even if it's information I've heard a hundred times. Maybe just getting out will help, and we can get some tea and talk too."

"I'd love to go, just to get out of the house for a few hours. Thanks."

As I shared out loud my concerns regarding Jasmine and her father, the parallel of me and my own father was quite glaring.

"You may want to talk with an attorney too," she said when I finished.

"Well, I don't want to do anything drastic or create more problems right now," I said. "I just need to know the law so I can make good decisions and feel peace of mind, making sure my concerns are addressed and properly written out, without making it all too complicated or difficult, the way I hear divorces and custody issues often are."

"Sounds like you need an attorney with a conscience, one who can help decide what is best for all of you."

"Yeah, right, like those exist."

Laughing, we enjoyed some time together before the workshop started. I was really glad I said yes to coming out with her, even though it was a Wednesday night. It was nice to be with her and share honestly what was on my mind. Just sitting in the auditorium was soothing. There was a peaceful energy surrounding the room. I exhaled deeper than I meant to.

Harpreete was right: Ron and Mary Hulnick's voices were soothing, and the seminar was entertaining and interesting. Invaluable. I was captivated hearing them speak what I read in the book. They spoke with such clarity that I *almost* enrolled in their Spiritual Psychology master's program myself.

Not now, I told myself. *It's not a good time. Maybe in the future. This program is exactly what I have been looking for, just not now. Too much going on to commit to this.*

"Thank you for joining us this evening," Ron Hulnick said. "We would like for one of our graduates to come up to share with you; please welcome Michael."

"Hello," the young man began. "My name is Michael Cotugno. I'm an attorney. I graduated from the University of Santa Monica a few years ago. I specialize in what I like to call conscious divorce and family law. I understand those two words seem like an oxymoron, but they are not. Not here."

I turned to Harpreete, speechless.

"I had no idea, I swear," she said; she took my hand as I began to cry.

Whatever teeny-tiny opening existed in the guarded shell around my heart, a spark of life entered.

God, knowing we were still not on speaking terms, still got my attention. I could not overlook this less than subtle hint, nudge, smack on the head.

You know you want to take this program at USM. You know it's exactly what you've been searching for, what you need. I heard my heart talking to me. Just as it did the morning the newspaper ad told me to take part in the Stanford University eating disorder study.

Fully aware of the events that transpired to bring me to this auditorium tonight and get my attention in this way, I listened. The unhealed part of my heart relating to my father screamed at me to finally face what I had not been wanting to or able to, until now. I knew it was time. And I accepted the call.

Chapter 42

Not long after moving in to our new place, there was a knock on the door.

"Hi, I'm Doug. We have a mutual friend in the building. He told me to come meet you, in case I need a good chiropractor."

Whoa. The energy of this six-foot, five-inch-tall frame, dazzling blue eyes, and beaming smile made every cell in my body oscillate. Where I lived, tall, handsome, athletic men were common, but none had this effect on me.

I politely extended one hand to greet Doug, keeping the other on my desk to stabilize my Jello legs. As his hand engulfed my shaking fingers, I spoke slowly as I introduced myself, hoping to gain some sense of control. He was here to meet a doctor, after all, not to be accosted by my runaway hormones.

As the door closed behind him, my legs gave way, the current emanating too much for me to control. I flopped into my chair to regain my composure; patients weren't scheduled for another hour. It took all that and then some to recover.

The following week, Doug popped his head in the door and said, "Hi, it's me. I don't need a chiropractor yet, I just wanted to come say hi."

What a fun surprise, I thought. "Come in." *Those blue eyes. Don't stare; it's creepy.*

Doug was surprisingly easy to talk with. He had a peaceful vibe, which made my nervousness subside (or at least it didn't appear so glaringly obvious). His energy was piercing; I felt almost relieved when he left.

I was delighted with the day's encounter; the surge of energy, along with the hint of his cologne, carried me to complete the backlog of overdue paperwork. I had not felt this rattled in years.

"Hi, again."

I raised my head from my desk to see the dazzling smile attached to the voice.

"I thought you might like some coffee. And maybe a croissant. Wasn't sure if you liked chocolate; I have both. And a bagel, in case you didn't like sweets."

I welcomed his kind offer with a goofy smile. For the next three hours, Doug listened intently and actively to my answers to the questions he asked. I was surprised at how easy he was to engage with; my nerves settled as we continued to laugh and share about ourselves.

As he stood up to leave, I smiled goodbye, silently wishing he would offer some kind of signal for me to know when I would see him again. But he didn't. I watched him go down the steps leading to the parking lot, but then he turned around and walked back up the stairs toward me.

He must have forgotten his keys or something, I thought.

"Hi, again," he began. "Would you like to have lunch with me sometime?"

"Yes, I'd love to," I said, my voice expressing more gusto than intended.

A Friday lunch date became a Friday dinner date. And Saturday dinner date. Consumed and infatuated, my head warned, *Don't get too attached, don't take him seriously.* My body shouted, "Go!" My heart whispered, "Why not?" So I leaped. I allowed myself to be carried away by the current. No longer interested in rationality, logic, or sense; my entire body, heart, and functional mind were devoured by hormones, ecstasy, and magic. The euphoria and fervor were intoxicating. I found myself conceding to agreements I normally would not make. Hypnotized, I found myself in a relationship where I squelched the subtle hints that emerged about his future plans. Despite my instincts, I thought the future of our relationship didn't matter. *I'll enjoy his company now*, I thought, *and see what happens later.* With school starting next week, I wouldn't have the same time and energy for him, anyway, so I decided to just enjoy the relationship the way it was.

Chapter 43

Sitting in the auditorium as a student was different than as a guest five months earlier at the University of Santa Monica. For the next two years, this was where I hoped to gain the information to help me let go of my past, my father, and whatever issues I had with him. I didn't know what the issues were, and I didn't know if USM could help, but I had to do this. I made a commitment to myself to finally get to the root of the anger I felt about him. I knew if I didn't deal with him, he'd continue to haunt me and mess up any and every intimate relationship I was in, whether it was with Doug or someone else. I was tired of carrying around the baggage of my father.

Opening weekend at USM, I knew I was in the right place, that I made the right decision to attend. I sat in a room with 250 others, unsure of how the next two years would go, but certain I needed to be there. I made myself comfortable and prepared for the ride.

Drs. Ron and Mary Hullnick wasted no time diving into the curriculum. Before the first hour concluded, a fundamental principle set the tone of my work: "If you're upset, it's your issue. Your feelings are never another person's fault. You are responsible for your feelings. Whatever you are feeling is going on inside of you. The other person simply triggers these feelings in you to surface, as an opportunity for you to become aware of them, to find the wound beneath the feeling, to heal it."

This was not the first time I heard these words, but it was the first time the concept applied to me. It was the first time I was struck by the simplicity and magnitude of this fundamental concept. It was the first day I felt I had control and a direction to finally take back the part of me my father hijacked, the part of me I thought untouchable since his death.

In this moment, I realized why Doug showed up in my life. He looked nothing like my father, yet his mannerisms and way of being triggering many of the same feelings of rage I felt about Dad. I saw that my behaviors and actions with Doug triggered feelings in me I didn't like and didn't want to face. But I knew I needed to. I understood the plan; for me to heal the wound of my father, I needed Doug to make them surface. I hated this; I hated both of them. I didn't want to do this, but I knew I had to.

With the kindness, compassion, and loving support of my classmates, I began pulling the threads of my unconscious, one by one bringing to the surface events, traumas, and circumstances of my past, dealing with situations with my father that paralyzed and controlled me.

Six months in, the conflicted feelings I experienced with Doug were too much for me to continue. I made the excruciating decision to end our relationship, although I felt deeply conflicted. I genuinely enjoyed Doug's company; I liked who he was. I enjoyed how we were together. My conflict was that our relationship had hit a ceiling; the future was in doubt. We had gone as far and as deep as he was willing to go. He was clear in his intention to not be in a relationship with more responsibility. I accepted his statements as true; I just didn't like them. Although I didn't like them, I accepted, and I stayed. But I no longer wanted to be in a relationship that felt limited.

I just did not want to say goodbye to the parts of our relationship that I loved, that were fun, that were intoxicating, that were fulfilling.

I truly enjoyed Doug as a person; I decided to remain friends, which seemed natural and appropriate.

Our friendship lasted ten days before our chemistry lured me back into an intimate relationship with Doug. This time, instead of being completely free with him, I felt tethered by embarrassment that I willingly agreed to return to this relationship, accepting the same terms. I felt ashamed of myself for accepting the same terms of the agreement, our previous arrangement that caused so much conflict in me.

I felt ashamed that the arrangement was not one I wanted for myself; it was not the kind of relationship I wanted for the long term. These were Doug's demands; I acquiesced to them because I liked him, maybe even loved him now.

The inner turmoil between who I wanted to be in relationship juxtaposed with the current relationship I was in let me know I had a lot of work to do to pry myself away from a toxic relationship. It was disguised by pleasure, attention, and affection; I accepted it as love.

Every weekend at USM, I slowly, willingly opened myself to the painful situation with Doug, allowing me to see the parallel of our relationship to the one with my father. I was on the right path to heal, which gave me inner strength and courage. I knew if I continued to do my work, the desperate feelings I exhibited with Doug would eventually melt away, freeing me to leave, completely.

Doug began to have health problems; we both knew it. I felt relieved to move into the arena of friendship once again; feelings of needing more subsided. I was tormented by the possibility of more still yearning in my heart; I decided once his health stabilized, once he focused attention on me again, maybe then we would continue.

Torn between wanting to walk away and not wanting to desert Doug as a friend. Not now, now while he focused on his health. Being a supportive friend cost me nothing. Months passed; Doug and I had the chance to become actual friends, a friendship where dating and sex didn't interfere. My head said this was a good place to be, a situation where I was free to date other men now. My heart acknowledged the circumstances, but I was unable to fully agree.

I was confused and crippled by my inability to pull my heart away from Doug; he seemed to accept the new terms of our friendship, without any need to change it. He seemed content. I felt dominated by a force compelling me to stay, to see what happened. As our friendship deepened, I was helpless, unable to date other men. My head said I should, that I was allowed to, but I declined all offers, as if accepting was a betrayal. To whom, I was not quite sure.

Every part of me wanted to run away from Doug. I was tormented with the desire to remain his friend during his time of need and the desperation to escape him. I didn't know what compelled me to stay. There was a familiar force haunting me, imploring me to stay. If I left, I felt condemned to repeat this cycle with a different man. If I stayed, I felt damned, damned that I would need to close my heart bit by bit in order to survive. My lacerated heart beat feebly. Every weekend at USM prodded my heart open to the pain I felt. I tried to circumvent the painful and uncomfortable feelings of hate, rage, and jealousy Doug triggered, finally acknowledging and accepting the truth. I needed to stare down the devil and face what I did not want to face.

I didn't like who I had become in this relationship. I didn't like who I had to be to remain in this relationship.

If I wanted out, I had to battle the voices in my head that forced me to stay. There was no other way.

Chapter 44

Dear Dad, Darnel Wilbur Nelson: I fucking hate you.

As a little girl, I always looked up at you in awe. You were so big, so tall, able to scoop me up with one arm, pulling me to your cheek for a kiss. Your booming laugh reverberated through every room in our house. Seeing your smile when you walked in my room made my heart crack open; I wanted to pour all the love my five-year-old heart could muster on you.

Your smile lit up every room we were in and every person you greeted. I wanted it all to myself. When you came home from work smelling of car grease and paint, I wanted to nestle up against you and jump on your back for a pony ride. Some days, you welcomed me into your arms, covering my face with kisses, delighted to see me. Most days, however, you swatted me away like a pesky mosquito. I should have listened; the tone of your voice hinted which side you would take. But I didn't listen. In my heart, I wanted the kind, loving, affectionate Daddy, so I ignored your warnings and ran into your arms.

I didn't understand your warnings. I was five; they were unclear to me. I didn't understand why you would hit my face so hard and shout at me to go away. I just wanted to show you how happy I was you were home. After you showered, you asked me to watch the news with you on the couch and to grab you a beer on the way.

I would give you your beer and run away to my room; I understand that warning sign. The sound of the fizzy froth escaping the can meant you would no longer be my funny, loving daddy. Your voice would change, and you yelled at Mom. I knew to stay in my room then.

I could hear your footsteps in the kitchen, the cabinet doors slamming so hard, the plates inside rattling. "Arlette, where's my whisky?" you would yell. "Where is my dinner?"

I'd curl up in a little ball and roll to the farthest corner beneath my bed, where your arms could not reach me. I wanted to muffle the sound of your voice; I didn't want to hear what came next, but I couldn't make it stop.

"Darnel, stop," Mom would say. "She's in the other room. You're hurting me."

I could hear the glass shatter on the kitchen floor. I heard you punching and kicking Mom as she cried for you to stop. Desperate for you to stop hurting her, I often ran into the kitchen. Sometimes, you stopped when you saw me. But sometimes, when you saw me, you'd grab my hand and spank me so hard on the back of my legs. You squeezed my arms together; the bones felt like they were being crushed.

I desperately wanted to save Mom. I knew that some days, you wore a belt in your work pants and took it out. You once hit me so hard, the belt buckle ripped my skin open; I got welts from the leather strap on my butt, arms, and back.

I didn't know what to do. I didn't know how to save Mom and keep us safe from you. I shut my eyes and covered my ears until her screams stopped, and then I fell asleep.

At breakfast the following morning, I sat at the table and said nothing, pretending I didn't hear anything last night. You kissed me and then left for work.

I remember one beautiful summer Saturday. You were outside working in the yard, and Mom was in the house. She shooed me out to play. I took my bike to Elizabeth's house next door, waving and calling, "I'll be home when the first street lights come on."

Elizabeth and I played in the orchards behind our block. Elizabeth and I could spend all day there, exploring. That day, she left to go home, but I wanted to stay longer and keep out of the house. As the sunlight dimmed, I made my way home, but my pant leg got caught in the bike chain. I was unable to stand or walk home; I sat on the curb, knowing you or Mom would come looking for me once the sun set and I wasn't home. So I sat still and waited.

I perked up when I saw your green pickup truck; you had arrived to save me. I knew you would rescue me. You unhooked my clothes, put my bike in the truck, and drove us home, telling me to shower and then come down for dinner.

When I came downstairs, you told me to stand by the banister and grab the wrought iron railing. Using your cloth dinner napkin, you tied my hands to the banister. While Mom and Grandmommy watched, you took your belt off and beat me so hard, I couldn't stand up. When Mom tried to intervene, you punched her and held the large kitchen knife to her face; you forced them to watch, warning them not to interfere, saying that I needed to be punished, to be taught a lesson about disobeying the rules. Beaten and bruised, I was sent to my room without dinner.

I don't understand, Daddy, I cried to myself. *Why did you do this to me? I'm only seven. I waited for you; I needed your help to get home. I waited for you; I don't understand what I did wrong. I don't know why you hurt me so much. I love you, Daddy; please stop hurting me. Please stop drinking beer and whisky; they make you hurt us. I wish you would stop; you scare me, Daddy.*

Holding my bear, I fell asleep.

Maybe you heard me. Maybe Mom heard me. You tried not to drink. I know you tried. And for all of fourth and fifth grade, I never went to school with another bruise.

But one day in sixth grade, as I came home from Elizabeth's house as the sun was setting, I could see two police cars in front of our house. I rushed to the door, and an officer put me in the back of his car, where Grandmommy was already sitting.

Dad was in handcuffs as they placed him in the second police car. Mom was talking with an officer as the car with Dad drove away. They let me and Grandmommy out of the car, and I rushed to Mom. She led me into the house, where I was confronted by the devastation within. Every plate, every glass, every item from the cupboards were smashed on the floor. Broken jars from the refrigerator oozed liquid among the destroyed dishware. The stuffing from the furniture had been ripped out, and the curtains were shredded in front of the sliding glass doors.

In my bedroom, every toy was destroyed, every stuffed animal's head was ripped off; stuffing was strewn across the floor. In Mom's closet, Dad had taken scissors to every item of clothing she owned, leaving shreds of fabric in a pile on the bed, among the smashed headboard and carved-up mattress.

I had no idea what happened; I looked at Mom and wondered how she could still be alive. Every inclination in my body told me if any of us had walked in while Dad was destroying our home, we most likely would not be alive. My fear of my father turned to terror.

That day was the final straw. Mom must have felt the same level of terror; she filed for divorce the next morning. I loved my dad but was relieved he was gone. I didn't know if I'd ever see him again, but I finally felt safe.

I wasn't sure where he was living, but he still called. It'd been over a year since he was taken away. I could tell Mom was hesitant to let him speak to me, but she allowed me to take the phone. I didn't know what to say. He said he was trying to stop drinking, but the sound in his voice exposed that as a lie. You promised to come see me on the weekend.

Every other Friday, you'd call, promising to see me the following day. I waited for you on the sidewalk with my bag of goodies and toys, but you didn't show up. I finally stopped believing you'd show up. The entire year of sixth grade, you never showed up.

One day, you finally came to take me to lunch. I was so excited to show you my new school and tell you about my new friends. I was bigger now and older. I no longer felt afraid that you'd hit me or hurt me. I could forgive you; you were there. We could start over.

At lunch, you told me about your new wife and your adopted stepkids: three boys. You discussed their activities and your involvement with their school functions. I showed you my volleyball schedule; you promised to come see me. You said you wanted to take me to lunch next month after a game. I accepted.

He seemed different, okay. Maybe his new wife was helping him get better. I repeated this over and over, as if saying it would somehow make it true, make me believe it was true, that you were a better dad now, that I could have the dad I loved back.

The next month, in the middle of our match, I saw his tall, slender frame enter the back door of the gym. *He showed up*, I thought. *My daddy showed up. It's true; he has changed.*

"Hi, kiddo," he said afterward. "Good game. You're growing and really look like a natural out there."

"Thanks, Dad. I'm glad you came. Where should we go for lunch?"

"The burger place around the corner is just fine."

I sat across from him in a booth; my heart was so full of love, so filled with joy that he showed up, that he came to see me, that even with his new family, I still mattered to him. Even if he hadn't been the best father, I still loved him. He was my dad, the only one I had. I was happy to see him.

To my delight, he wanted to have lunch again next month, even if we didn't make it to payoffs. I promised to call him with the news and schedule; either way, we could have lunch together. I sent him off with the biggest hug my arms could squeeze around him. The love in my heart once again poured all over him.

I knew he made mistakes; he knew he made mistakes, although we never talked about the past. He was trying. Mom said she forgave him; I could too. Mom said she liked that we had lunch together, so I felt good about our time. She seemed happier now than she had ever been. The divorce had been good for everyone.

But the next month, after waiting three hours and calling his home, I realized Dad wasn't coming. We finished our playoff match; we lost. The season was done. I called Mom to pick me up at the gym; everyone else had long gone home.

Mom didn't say anything in the car; I was grateful for the silence. I should have known better. I knew it was too good to be real. I didn't think he could ever hurt me again, but he still found a way to break my heart. Maybe it would be better if I just didn't have a father, if I just pretended he went away for good. That way, I'd never have to go through this pain again, never give Dad a way to hurt me. *From now on*, I thought, *I don't have a father. I disown him.*

I no longer wanted to be Darnel's daughter. I hated him. I'd better off if he were dead. I'd never allow myself to be in this position again, never allow myself to be hurt like this, never allow myself to be ambushed again. Never again would I open my heart to a man, give him the power to hurt me. Never again would I allow myself to be vulnerable to you. Never again would I let my guard down. I promised myself.

So much hurt, anger, regret, and rage spewed out of me. I knew my father could hear me. I held a photo of my father; the damaged, broken little girl inside of me was finally able to speak. She finally had a voice to speak up and say all that she had been holding in.

She was finally free to speak, and I was finally able to hear what she had to say:

"I love you, Dad, but I want nothing to do with you. I'm tired of making excuses for you, making up reasons why you didn't show up to be with me. I'm tired of being on the receiving end of your bad behavior, wrenching my gut, ripping my heart open, for all the promises you never kept.

"You came to my high school graduation, but it was too late. There was too much resentment, too much rage, too much sorrow, but I promised myself I would never feel sad about you, ever again. Day-to-day requires so much energy from me; I can't allow any sadness to interfere with my life. I wish you were dead so I could be free of you.

"I still love you, but I wish I didn't have a father, at least not you as my father. I love you, but I hate that when you came home, I didn't know if you were going to hug me or beat me. I had to be afraid of my own father. I shouldn't have been terrified of you. I shouldn't have been afraid in my own home, wondering if you were going to ambush me or Mom and terrorize us. I hate you for making me feel unsafe in my home. I hate that I had to learn how to protect myself from you, when all I wanted was to play with you. I hate that I was too little to protect myself from you, that I had to learn how to hide my vulnerability, to not let you catch me unguarded.

"I still love you, Dad. And I hate you. You are still my dad; I cannot change that. You are the only dad I'll ever have. I am fine without you. I will be fine without you. I have no need for you. I want nothing to do with you. I cannot escape from you. I wish I didn't look like you. I wish people would stop telling me how much I remind them of you. I can't completely rid myself of you, but I can ignore you.

"You are dead to me. Everything that you are is dead to me. I made sure to bury everything about me that resembles you, cleansing myself of you. When signs of you appeared, when I could no longer contain the pain of you or keep the pain buried, I soothed myself with food. When I could not eat to make you disappear, alcohol would numb me. I could drink you away.

"I continued my life without you. I learned how to function and survive without you. I felt the pang in my heart of longing for you to call, to see how my day was and share with me yours. I missed you when the little girl in me looked around while playing volleyball, to see if I could catch a glimpse of you. My heart aches knowing you are not there. I longed for you when the little girl in me wanted to feel you kiss my cheek, hug me close, and tuck me in bed. To hear you laugh with me, your booming smile lighting up my world, one more time. Sitting on the edge of your hospital bed, I wanted so much to tell you I love you and forgive you, but I couldn't. Seeing you, knowing alcohol caused you to deteriorate, that you allowed it to take you away, again, this time for good, was too much for me to understand and face, so I didn't.

"There was a hole in my heart in the shape of my father; nothing could heal the pain. The rage, guilt, and shame of you festered in me, rotting every part of me that was like you.

"You were my dad, you were supposed to keep me safe, protect me, care for me, adore me, want me, love me."

None of that mattered after he died; I let all of those feelings stay buried, tucked away, never to be felt again. Until I met Doug. And then my heart began to crack open. As my heart began to open to him, all the feelings I had buried about you came rushing to the surface, and I hated you all over again. I hated Doug for making these feelings surface. I hated not knowing what to do with them, how to handle them, how to make them go away.

The more my heart opened with Doug, the more I was flooded by the painful experiences of my dad. Thirty-five years of hatred, rage, jealousy, envy, anguish, guilt, shame, grief, confusion, defeat, disappointment, brokenness, damage, worthlessness, powerlessness, disbelief. For thirty-five years, I managed to contain these uncomfortable, painful feelings. And all at once, they oozed out, toxic, gangrenous; pus oozed from my heart and every cell in my body that held a memory of him.

I could no longer bury him; while I may be able to survive, I could not thrive in a life I wanted with him haunting me.

So here we are, Dad, I thought. *Finally ready to allow you in my life, in a way that is honest.*

I may not yet know what or how that looks, but I was ready to accept him, the broken father he was, as my dad. I still loved him, but today, I hated him a little less than yesterday.

I released myself from the strangle of my father. I felt myself becoming free. Something in me had changed, though I was not sure exactly what. The world looked the same; I felt the same, but the reflection in the mirror looked different.

I met with Doug the following day. I was finally able to end our intimate relationship. I saw how Doug and I had recreated the emotional patterns of my father: the push-pull, love-hate, break up and make up. I was unable to break off my connection with him because the relationship I had with Doug felt familiar. I didn't like it, but it was familiar. Doug triggered in me all of the uncomfortable experiences and pain, driving me to act out, not knowing how else to cope. The place in me that was hurting from my dad was beginning to heal. Giving a voice to the part of me that was hurting, instead of trying so much to suppress it, gave me the strength to let go of the dysfunctional part of the intimate relationship I had with Doug. The parts of Doug I genuinely liked, I wanted to keep in my life. His kind, gentle, loving friendship was a gift, a gift I accepted from him.

As I began to accept my father, I began to accept the parts of me that were just like him. While the hole in my heart was not gone, I'd taken the toxins out and gave the wound a good rinsing with the saline of tears. I knew the wound would heal in time, but a scar would remain.

Chapter 45

One day, I when I went over to Mom's, I noticed some bruising on her cheeks.

"Mom, what happened?" I asked. "How did you get that bruise on your face?"

The raccoon bruising pattern around both her eyes smacked me in the gut.

"It's nothing," she said. "I wasn't paying attention when I was walking the dog and tripped on a piece of raised sidewalk. It looks worse than it is."

"It likes like your face hit the ground. Did you go to the doctor?"

"Yes, my eyes are fine; the brain scan was negative. Really, it looks worse than it feels. I'm more embarrassed than anything."

Mom was so independent, always has been "a tough cookie," as she called herself. She was getting older, and I saw her doing so much every day. I hoped she was not pushing beyond her physical ability. She worked many different jobs, some for social connection, most to support herself. Although she only lived a few miles from me, I worried about her. There were a number of incidents that reminded me of her age and limitations.

I, too, was feeling financial pressure. As health care policies continued to change, insurance was no longer dependable to sustain my practice; each month, the business was in a deficit. Credit cards and bank loans kept the business operating now.

I knew Mom was upset about the financial instability I put myself in with the divorce, but she accepted that the decision was best for me. She was the reason I was able to complete the master's program and continue to survive as a single parent. I could see how much she adored Jasmine. I often envied how much fun she had making plans with Jasmine; she cared for her and spent time with her, the way I wish she had paid attention to me. Jasmine was the beneficiary of Mom's kinder, gentler self, softer Mom. I was happy for her. With me, it was just business as usual. Our conversations rarely extended beyond day-to-day operations, pick-up, drop-off, and how I was doing with work.

I didn't know what I was doing with work now. I wasn't sure I wanted to work as a chiropractor any longer. It'd been fifteen years in LA, and I was tired of operating this business. Inside Out Wellness Center had consumed so much of my life. I wanted a change, but didn't have the courage to leave and do what I really wanted. I wanted to write and facilitate workshops. I knew with my first public speaking engagement to promote Inside Out that this was my calling. Speaking about health and wellness, sharing the information I learned for myself, and sharing my heart was exactly what I wanted to do. But I just couldn't seem to put the pieces in place to make a viable career and business with it.

I'd tried, unsuccessfully, to recreate the workshops I once offered, but with my divorce, school, and work, everything consumed all my resources. I was a single mom; I couldn't make another life-altering change that would affect both Jasmine and me, if I failed. Quitting chiropractic would be selfish, too destructive to consider, just to follow some wild dream. It'd been eighteen years. I couldn't change directions now; it was what I knew. This was what I was good at. This was what I was meant to do.

Currently, my business was stagnant, and with Mom getting older, I needed to be concerned with caring for the three of us.

One day, we were talking in my kitchen; I said, "You know, Mom, it would be easier for me to focus on rebuilding the business, take care of Jasmine, and keep an eye on you if you were living here with us. Just think about it; if moving in with us is something you'd like, let me know."

I don't think I even completed my sentence before she answered. "Yes," she said. "I want to."

I was relieved to have her with me, with us. I could focus attention on work; the office had downsized again, to a single room, a small office space. It was time to focus and rebuild. I was apprehensive about the impact having Mom living with us in our small apartment, but we'd figure it out. Less than ideal, Jasmine's wish for a cat on her seventh birthday came as a complete package: a cat, a dog, and a grandma. It was cozy and hopefully temporary, until I could rebuild the business and move us into a larger place.

While playing in a game one day, I heard "Pop!" It sounded like a single shot fired.

It was the sound, I was told, a ligament makes when it ruptures: a sound I'd never heard, until then.

The four of us on the volleyball court all heard the single shot. I collapsed on the sand, clutching my left knee. Fear gripped me more than pain. I cried as I watched the fluid begin to accumulate. Afraid of the worst-case scenario, a torn ACL, I made myself get up and go home immediately. Hobbling on one leg as my friends carried me home, flashes of the next six to nine months of rehabilitation and downtime following surgery fired at rapid speed through my mind: *How the fuck am I going to work? What will this mean for us? I can't be hurt; I can't afford to be hurt. I've never been hurt.*

With an ice machine compressing my knee, I called my colleagues and friends, an orthopedic surgeon and a physical therapist; I prepared for what was to come.

Maybe God was telling me something, trying to get my attention. I may not really believe in you, God, but I know when to listen.

There was nothing more I could do on this holiday Monday. My recovery plan was in place, organized with my home therapy machines and appointments tomorrow; no matter what the diagnosis was, I was prepared. I needed to squelch my racing, nervous mind; I looked at my notes from a seminar I attended two days earlier, trying to use my time to create a work plan for a new workshop. *Okay, God,* I thought. *I'll work harder.*

The next morning, I surveyed the overnight damage; the swelling was at its peak. It was not as bad as I thought it would be. Maybe it was not serious, after all. But when I stepped gingerly with my good leg out of bed to steady myself, and then shifted my weight to the left.

"Oh, fuck!" I yelped.

The sensation of a knife stabbing the bone in my leg dropped me back on my bed. Lying on my back, my fat knee was discolored. Something was definitely wrong.

I needed to keep it immobile, so the swelling could go down. There was time for physical therapy before my appointments. It didn't feel so bad. I tried again to get out of bed.

With my knee iced, brace tight, I made it to the kitchen, albeit slowly and wobbly, but I hobbled around. This was good. I was going to be okay. I didn't think surgery would be required, but I wasn't ruling it out yet. The long-term integrity of my knee was too valuable. I had to be able to work; I needed my whole body to do adjustments. This was the first time my work ability had ever been compromised. I decided to take this injury seriously.

The surgeon concurred after examining me; he said, "Your knee is surprisingly stable. I don't believe you fully tore the ACL, just a sprain. Surgery is not required, unless you don't rehabilitate properly."

His ironic smile mocked me.

"Check in with me once the swelling goes down," he concluded, "and we can determine the next best step for you."

I was grateful for his honesty; he'd been a great surgeon to my patients through the years. There was no need to doubt his assessment.

My rehabilitation plan was in effect. Without volleyball, there was a lot more free time in my day. I used this time to figure out my next steps for work, business, and career. I knew I was on borrowed time with my office. Each month, I was digging myself into a deeper hole financially. I had to come up with a sustainable solution if I was going to salvage this practice.

My knee gave me permission to slow down. It intuitively knew I had been pushing my body in extreme; my luck was not an oversight by me. My body, resilient in its health, had bent in many unkind directions; I had wielded it without breaking. It was time for me to take better care of it. This was just a warning sign. I needed to restructure my energy and resources.

Honestly, I was not surprised. I had not stopped since I went back to chiropractic school in 1997, almost twenty years now. The responsibilities of business combined with marriage, divorce, motherhood, and an aging parent consumed me. All of my energy was squeezed out, leaving me surviving on fumes. I was exhausted, completely depleted, and burned out. I was desperate to salvage my practice, my business; it was all I had for us.

I had to go on; it was all on me to figure this out, to figure out my life. I needed a workable plan to get myself out of this mess I created. It was just me; I had to find a way to fix this. My knee was just the first sign that the way I was living was unsustainable. I knew this.

Twenty years with patients had given me the opportunity to see firsthand how the physical body revealed signs and symptoms to get our attention, to draw our awareness to the parts that needed additional support, whether the needs were nutritional in nature, sleep deprivation, or any ailment of stress or dis-ease, anything emotional.

I learned after seeking personal information from patients that the parallel was unmistakable: the mind and body connection. For most of the past five years, my physical body had been running on fumes, the fumes of depletion, from going in all directions in my life, fully engaged, two feet in, without really assessing, I mean really assessing the direction I was going. Just nose to the grindstone and go.

My knee problem physically slowed me down; my awareness was opening up to the not-so-subtle hint that moving forward in the same way, on the same path, was the wrong move. Emotionally, I was ready for a change; I just didn't know how to make the changes I wanted. I secured three nutrition and health workshops for the following month; I believed this was the answer, the direction to go in, that would lead me to my dream career. I had a plan, and with effort, it seemed to be moving along.

One beautiful February morning, I had a workshop scheduled that evening with twenty-five attendees. Reworking my content for the past month, I was prepared, excited, and ready. My knee felt stronger, more stable; I was able to walk in the soft sand. It was a perfect way to start the day.

I felt mildly off-center through the walk; the pressure in my head was more pronounced with each step. I cut the walk short, returning home to eat and rest. My simple comforting brunch was unusually filling that morning. I lay back on the couch, my head spinning; after a minute, ignoring the pain in my knee, I launched myself into the bathroom, opening the door with just enough time to hurl into the toilet. The spinning escalated as the fever made its presence known. Chills, condensation accumulating on my forehead, swirling stomach; ugh.

Food poisoning? Maybe; the eggs didn't taste funny, but it was possible. *Fuck!* I thought. *Why today? There's no way I am cancelling the workshop. I don't want to disappoint the organizer or the attendees.*

I can't afford to look bad on the first day of my new life's direction. No way. I am going. I can rest tomorrow.

I sought the strength to present a workshop I could feel proud of, but then I collapsed into bed. I woke the following morning with a fever of 104 degrees; I couldn't deny what my body was telling me: This was not food poisoning; this was the flu. More than twenty years had passed since I last had the flu. I couldn't remember what the flu was like. I knew my body was taxed, but I didn't know it was that depleted.

I lay in bed for ten days, unable to work or move beyond the bathroom; my body took the rest it needed and craved, the rest I had been depriving myself of.

Being unable to work forced myself to think; it was almost worse than the flu itself. Each day I spent in bed was another day without working, without an income. One day closer to losing everything.

With nowhere to go, I was left with the voices in my head: *What are you going to do? If you don't work, you could lose everything, You're already on the edge; this is going to push you over. Then what are you going to do? How will you survive? How will you take care of Mom and Jasmine? Even if you find a job at the local grocery store, the salary won't pay the rent. Where will you live? What will happen to you, to your family? Everything is depending on you; you're responsible for your family.*

"I don't know!" I screamed into my pillow when the house was silent. "I don't know. Stop talking; leave me alone. I don't know what I'm going to do."

I really didn't know what the fuck to do. I barely had the strength to stay afloat before getting sick and getting injured. Now I faced the daunting, impossible task of making up for lost time and lost money; my dreams were no longer a vision I could hold onto. I needed to put all my focus on chiropractic; it was the only feasible direction to crawl out from beneath the financial cage I put myself in.

No part of my body wanted to get up and continue, but I had no choice. I had to. I was a mother; I was responsible for too much.

My dreams no longer mattered. Survival was all that mattered now. At my current pace, if the finances didn't drastically improve in the upcoming months, I was facing the harsh reality of moving. *Get moving*, the sergeant in my head commanded. *No time to be weak; no time for pity. You made this fucked-up mess; you fix it.*

I got out of bed, put on my big girl pants, and went out. What I felt didn't matter. What I dreamed didn't matter. Nothing mattered now, except to survive. I put my best smile on so no one knew the truth of what was happening. Above all, I let no one know of my dire situation. I smiled my biggest, brightest, happiest smile so no one would know.

I used every marketing and promotion tactic that brought any success in the past eighteen years, hoping to kick-start the practice back to life; I invested every dollar left to my name, every particle of energy remaining in my body. There was barely a perceptible bump on the Richter scale after three months. Disbelief turned to terror as my efforts yielded no results. My savings were now completely drained, my retirement accounts emptied, all credit cards carrying maximum balances, in an effort to salvage my practice, my life.

The tyrant in me screamed its demands: "Do more! You have to work harder. You have to do something else. You're not working hard enough. You are failing. You're the reason the business is failing. You need to push harder, give more, sacrifice more, figure it out. Do whatever you need to do to make it work. You have nothing left. The end is close. If you can't make this happen, you will lose everything."

I was exhausted by the terror of not knowing what to do; my resources were exhausted. Hearing the crickets chirping through the night, I continued to function on fumes.

I don't know what to do, what more I can do, I said to myself.

My heart knew I was pouring every resource I had into the business, trying to survive. My head, looking at the financials, couldn't believe I was doing enough.

One night, I was jolted awake by a stabbing pain in my lower back. The gripping pain forced me to fall back on my bed. I couldn't move; the shearing pain stabbed me with such force, rendering me unable to move. I didn't remember hurting myself. What the fuck was going on? Did I rupture an organ? Was I passing a kidney stone? Holy shit; whatever this was, I couldn't move.

I called out to Mom, "I don't know what's going on. I need help to get out of bed and use the bathroom."

I moved my leg for Mom to close the bathroom door for privacy, but after she did, the intensity of the pain was so fierce, I fell off the toilet and lost consciousness. I came to after I hit my head on the bathroom wall. The intense pain in my back forced me to stay on the floor, unable to move. Eventually, my seventy-year-old mom and seven-year-old daughter did their best to help me back into bed.

"Mom, I'm scared," I said. "I don't know what's happening. If the pain doesn't settle down in a few hours, I need to go to the hospital."

I had never been this afraid about my body or health. This kind of pain rivalled childbirth, but not knowing the cause amplified the distress. I trembled in bed, my imagination terrorizing me.

As long as I didn't move and stayed completely still on my back, I didn't feel any pain. That was a good sign, I thought, trying to convince myself, to come off the imaginary death bed I was on. I didn't have a fever, just the sweat caused by pain. That was a good sign too. I didn't need to go to the hospital, I didn't want to deal with the hospital. I decided to wait a few more hours.

I lay, motionless on my back, the sheets wet from perspiration. Pain was mixed with the sweltering June heat in my room. I could have moved to a dry spot on the sheets but chose not to, afraid to awaken the tormentor in my lower back.

I was able to keep the tormentor at bay; the tyrant, however, had full reign in my mind.

Now what are you going to do? I asked myself. *You have enough money to pay rent for July, and that is it. August first, you need to pay either rent at home or your office rent; you won't be able to pay both. It will be all gone unless you get out of bed right now and do something.*

I was unable to move, unable to do something or do more; the voice in my mind had me captured, unable to escape its relentless rant:

If you had not been so selfish, filing for divorce, you wouldn't be in this mess. If you hadn't been so stupid, you wouldn't have botched up your business. If you hadn't been so lazy, you wouldn't be in trouble now. If you hadn't been so careless and so naive, your life wouldn't be in such shambles today. You really fucked up, and there are serious consequences to pay now. If you cannot make rent, you will lose your home. You will be the reason that you, Mom, and Jasmine are homeless. You are the reason your daughter will be taken away from you. It will be all your fault. You really are too stupid to deserve her. This is what you get.

Chapter 46

Oh, God, I thought, *I don't know what to do. I am terrified, and I am at a loss. I really don't know what to do anymore. I really messed up. I can't get out of bed. I can't go to work. I can't take care of my family, the only people that really matter to me. I am so scared. I don't know what else to do, where to go from here. I don't know how to come back from this and make everything right again.*

"You don't," the whispering voice in my head answered.

But I have to.

"But you can't."

I don't know what to do, I replied, conceding defeat.

"I know you don't."

I can't see a way out of this mess. I don't know how to get myself, my family, out.

"You can see the answer; you just don't like the option that's left."

I can't close the business. I can't lose everything. I can't just quit and allow everything to disappear.

"Why not?"

Because this business is all I have. This office, Inside Out, is all I know. This practice, being a chiropractor, is all I know how to do. If I allow it to fall apart, I will have nothing, I am nothing.

The battle in me, in my head, ceased for a moment. The winner, undecided.

"Are you ready now?"

Ready for what? My agitation was clear.

"Ready to stop fighting. Ready to listen. Ready to trust?"

No, but I don't think I have a choice right now, do I?

"You have a choice; you just don't like it."

Well, I'm too tired to fight. I have nowhere to go, so I'll listen. But I'm not sure I can trust.

"You don't need to trust. But you came to me. Can you tell me why you don't want to trust me? Why are you unable or unwilling to trust me?"

You're kidding, right? You seriously need me to tell you why I don't trust you? Why I can't trust you? If you are all knowing, then you should know.

"I do know. I want you to tell me, so I can hear directly from you, and we can talk about it. We can have an open conversation about anything you're thinking or feeling about me. I promise you: There is nothing you can say I don't already know. Nothing you can say I haven't heard before. Nothing you can say we cannot talk about. Every time you need me, you call me, so you have to trust me a little. If you are honest with yourself right now, you can see that when you have called on me, I've been here for you."

Yes, but only when my situation was dire did you show up.

"That's because you only called on me when you were in a desperate situation. I was there before. You just didn't want to listen. I've always been with you; you just couldn't hear me. I know you are angry at me. You don't understand me. Since you have nowhere to go, how about we talk now? How about you just let me hear whatever you have to say, need to say to me?"

Since you seem so intent on hearing what I have to say, are you ready?

"I am ready; go ahead."

Fuck you, God!

Chapter 47

How's that for starters?

"Keep going; let it all out."

I believe in you. I just don't trust you. I want to trust you. I wish I could trust you; I just don't think I can. Yes, you show up in my desperate hour, but not always. Yes, you've helped guide me, but I cannot count on you to always show up. You are inconsistent; sometimes, you show up to help. Sometimes, you don't. I cannot trust your inconsistent nature. I cannot rely on you, not fully. When you show up, you are amazing, the greatest source of support, strength, and guidance. But you are fickle. You contradict yourself; you're situation-dependent. Your temperamental, mercurial ways make me suspect you, your intentions, your supposed authority, certainly the disparate ways you show love to your perceived favorites. But above all, your judgments.

Silence.

I knew you couldn't handle what I had to say to you, about you.

"I am here. I am listening. I know you have more to say. I didn't want to interrupt. Keep going. I know you are holding back, afraid. Let it all out. I can take it."

When I was hiding in my closet, scared that Dad was going to kill Mom, where were you? When Dad held me down and beat the shit out of me, where were you? I was five years old. If you knew all that was happening, why did you allow it to continue? When I was seven and Dad found me in the back of my closet, dragging me out, I called to you. You were not there to protect me while Dad made Mom watch as he viciously unleashed his rage on me, then turned on her.

Where were you when Mom and I were homeless, sleeping on the floor of Elizabeth's room? I could hear Mom crying, fearing for our survival. Remember me crying to you, calling to you? Well, you didn't come to help. You weren't there. And now you want me to trust you? Fuck you. Fuck no!

"I'm still here, listening. I know you have more you want to say to me. It's okay; say whatever comes up, everything that you have been holding in. Set it free."

In my heart, I wanted so much to give you another chance; Mom did. After we moved, she found comfort in you. What I found was more contention. My hatred of you only grew more intense, listening to the pastor tell me I was bad, I was born bad, a sinner. I was born flawed and should be ashamed of my flaws and everything about me that was bad. Remember the pastor telling Mom she should be ashamed of herself for selling her soul and damaging mine by sending me to a Catholic school, instead of the Christian school? That you, God, would condemn us for allowing me to be corrupted and educated by teachers unworthy of the honor to teach. I remember the words from you, Pastor, the man of God, you appointed to the church Mom trusted. Mom remained faithful to you, trusting you. I could not.

Remember, God, I looked for you in the school church, hoping to find you. And there, I was told by the priest that I should be ashamed of who I was, ashamed to be the child of a mother who chose to divorce my father, who chose to break her vow of marriage. That when Mom chose to be faithful to you in her church, the Catholic church rescinded our tuition assistance, to condemn us. Do you remember the priests, the men you chose to share your word? I was looking for you, and this was what I received from you. You make me sick.

The only reason I believe in you is because when I look at the human body, I am overcome with awe. There is much more than science can see or explain about the wonder of the human body and the universe. Each advancement science makes only seems to confirm what already exists, that science, math, and technology are only able to look at, to study, not to create. I see how the human body just repairs itself when given the proper environment. I see how an entire human is created from two cells. For me, the only reason, I still believe in you is from looking at the cadavers in anatomy lab, knowing that at one time, they were alive, breathing and eating, maybe even laughing and loving. And to see their corpse, with no life force flowing, I knew there had to be more than just a collection of cells that through happenstance found their way to function together. When I cut the cadaver open, and he didn't bleed, intuitively, I knew it was you that no longer existed in him. That you were that force of energy that made life possible.

But I still don't understand you or trust you.

You say that my human desires, my human needs, make me a bad person, a human being that you judge as disgusting, as repulsive. Well, you fucking made me. Why the fuck would you make me and then tell me everything about me is bad and wrong, that I should be ashamed of the way you made me? What kind of Father are you? You are not the kind, loving, gentle father that Mom, the pastors, and all the people in this church claim you to be. I trust the life force in me, not you.

"So you believe in this life force, a force you cannot see, hear, smell, taste, or touch? What would you call this life force in you?"

Energy, life, universal intelligence, spirit; any of these terms work for me.

"Do you think it is possible that the life force, universal intelligence, spirit, energy that you acknowledge is me, with a different name?"

I'm not sure. I never allowed myself to consider that idea as a possibility.

"Who do you think you are talking to right now?"

Myself. Just me having a conversation with me, in my head.

"Who do you think is with you, engaging in these conversations with you, participating in the questioning with you and listening to you with complete attention?"

Me.

"That's right. You. You, when you are being totally honest and completely candid about what you are feeling in your heart, that is you; that is me. You can call It God, but you seem to prefer other words, so pick whichever one you like, and we can use whatever you're comfortable with.

"I am still here, listening. Are you there?"

I'm here. I just don't have anything else to say.

"You said a lot. Thank you for trusting me to share every feeling you had in your heart. Thank you for the courtesy of telling me everything that you felt confused and angry about. Thank you for sharing your most personal and painful interactions with me. I have more for you, answers to your deepest, heartfelt questions, questions that deserve to be answered honestly. I will answer them all."

I turned to pull the sheets over me. I held my breath, preparing for the searing pain in my back to assault me. Conscious of the noticeable lack of pain when I moved, I began to cry. Feeling light-headed, I closed my eyes; my weary body needed rest.

I was awakened by Jasmine, jumping on the bed and saying, "Are you going to be okay, Mommy?"

"You know what, baby?" I replied. "I am going to be okay."

"Do you need to go to the hospital?" Mom asked.

"No, I think I'm really going to be all right."

With Jasmine tucked in bed beside me, Mom's lights were out in her room, although I knew she was not asleep. I turned my light on and took out my journal.

Okay, God, spirit, universal intelligence, life force, energy, whatever the fuck you go by. I am listening too. I can accept you exist. I don't really understand you, but I acknowledge you. I don't know you, but I am willing to find out. I believe in you. Today, I trust you more than I did yesterday. I know you have been trying to get my attention, trying to get me to listen. I am ready now. I am here now. Not trying to negate our progress, but I need some answers before I can move forward. Before I can completely trust you, I need to know how the fuck I ended up here. Help my mind understand so my heart can open; that's the order I work in. it is the only way I know to really see the mistakes I made in order to understand how to avoid making them again. Do we have a deal?

"Take out your journal, open your mind, and open your heart. Start writing. I will give you the answers you seek."

Chapter 48

"How the fuck did I end up here?" Big letters were draped along the top on the page. Confusion whirled; I wondered what egregious mistakes I made that I did not see at the time. The rage subsided, leaving me open, curious. Abstain my belligerence with spirit and willing to hear, my heart opened to know the truth of how I found myself in this mess. Where did I go wrong? I knew I was responsible for all of the choices, decisions, actions, and behaviors that led me to this point. I knew it was my fault. I just wished I knew what I did wrong. Where did I go astray? I did everything I knew how to do, to the best of my ability, but this was where I landed.

I was out of commission for an entire week from my back episode; when I got up, I prepared myself to survey the damage. Without working for a week, the delicate pulse on my business told me the time was coming for tough choices to be made. Care for my current patients took all my energy. I spent a few hours a day at the office and the remaining hours of the day was in bed, sleeping, unable to muster the energy to play volleyball or go for a walk. I didn't have the energy to engage with Jasmine or Mom. All I wanted to do was sleep, disconnect from the entire world and let it all come crashing down. I was tired of trying to hold up my life, to keep it going, tired of trying to make it work. Beyond tired or drained: depleted, exhausted; I had nothing left.

I was bankrupt: emotionally, physically, spiritually; all but financially. I had nothing to give to anyone. Not myself, not my child, nothing. I pushed my body past the redline, using fumes to keep me afloat. I gave myself permission to crash.

Facing life-altering decisions, I needed space to think, to process all that transpired. At home, Mom's constant glare followed my every move. Feeling her condescending, critical eyes, I stayed in my room, coming out only when she was gone. Once my immediate health threat passed, Mom made little effort to hide her disgust at my lackluster desire to get back to work.

I knew there was no more work to do. I had three weeks left until I made a formal announcement. The choice had already been made for me; I had just not yet accepted it yet. I had not yet processed the magnitude of what was happening; it was too big to fully wrap my mind around it and face the truth, along with the consequences.

Twelve years had passed since I last had time away from work. A road trip with Jasmine would do me some good. I needed to come up with a plan of what's next.

First stop, overnight at a friend of twenty-three years; it was always fulfilling to spend time with her. I made my way up the coast; Monterey was a beautiful stop, perfect for a few days with another friend of twenty years. I headed out across the bay and stopped in my former hometown, a last-minute gift: Dominic. Facebook kept us acquainted with one another, never more than a friendly hello. An exchange of kind, loving words, twenty-five years overdue, from the day I stormed off the basketball court. Onward to my cousin's house for a few more days.

Clarity and peace of mind were still eluding me.

Sixteen years ago when I left San Jose, I didn't take the time to say goodbye to the life I had. I just left, anxious to leave behind the life I wanted to escape from. A brief Facebook exchange reconnected me with another friend I had left behind. For five years, my workout partner, buddy, friend, was a constant in my life, until I just walked away, leaving our friendship behind. I found out he lived less than a mile from my cousins. I made time to see him and complete what I left behind.

I spent a few days with my cousins, rounding off a ten-day trip. It was 4:30 a.m., and Jasmine was sleeping in the back seat as I made my way onto Interstate 5. Sixteen years ago, my heart filled with possibility and joy as Journey kept me company. This morning, the forceful voice of Josh Groban was playing, highlighting the purple, pink, orange, and yellow hues of the sun kissing the early morning sky, luring out the contents of my broken heart. Today, the confusion in my mind rendered me unable to think rational thoughts at the daunting prospect of facing what awaited at home.

Reflecting on friends and family of the past ten days, an odd sensation overwhelmed me. It was as if I had the chance to say goodbye to some important people from my life. If something were to happen to me, at least the final memory they'd have of me would be good.

In three days, I would be taking the final course of action that would seal the fate of my office. I had exactly enough money to pay for one month of rent, either home or office, not both. I was able to pay rent for a home for one more month, and that was it. I still hadn't figured out a plan. I still didn't know what I was going to do. One absolute certainty I knew for sure:

God, I am sorry. I fucked up and don't know how to get out of this mess. I am too tired to fight. I will not live without my child. If I find myself in a situation where she's taken from me, I will execute my plan to take both our lives. I refuse to live without her and have her taken from me for my failures, my inability to care for her, support her, and provide for her. If suicide is my only way out, I'll do it. I don't want to die. I just don't want to live like this anymore. If I can't figure out how to function in this world, I no longer want to be a part of it. I don't know what's happened to me. I know I'm on the brink of losing everything, and I cannot get myself out of bed to get a job. All of my fight is gone. All of my ability to pull myself up is gone. The scrappy fighter, the survivor, the warrior, the do-whatever-it-takes person is gone. She is gone, and I don't know how to get her back. She is gone, and I cannot live without her. She's been the force that has pulled me out of every mess in my life. She's been with me since I hid in the closet at five years old. She's gone, and without her, I lack the fortitude to start over again. She is gone; I am gone. She is dead; I am dead.

My defender, my conqueror, my guardian is gone. Without her, I don't know how to function in this world. My champion, protector, and heroine vanquisher has kept me alive, helped me soldier through this world. Without her, I'm unable to survive the consequences of the mess I created. If I feel the need to take my life, I will take Jasmine with me.

Chapter 49

On Sunday, August 1, 2016, Inside Out Wellness Center officially closed. I carried the boxes out one at a time, along with the furniture, dumping them on my courtyard, the reality coming into focus. It was gone. It's over. The thirty-day countdown began; if I didn't have a viable financial solution, I wouldn't be able to pay rent for September. My family would be homeless.

I'm a failure, an inept mother, unable to provide for my child. My worst fear is coming true: the terrorizing reality that my child can be taken from me. The result of my failure and inadequacies as a business owner and combination of my irreparable damage by my inability to force myself to find a way out. I know what I'm experiencing is true, but I feel disconnected from the reality. Too withdrawn to fully comprehend the magnitude of my world crumbling.

Everything I've worked to achieve for over twenty years is gone. As if none of my efforts mattered, as if my heart that I poured into chiropractic did not matter. Nothing I sacrificed to succeed mattered; I didn't succeed. None of the resources, no matter how much time, money, sweat equity, tears I gave to Inside Out, none of it mattered. All I had to offer, I gave, and none of what I had to give mattered. It was as if the past twenty years of my life didn't matter. My work, the service I provided, the care I provided, none of it mattered. My heart that I gave to the office didn't matter.

Too numb to decide what to do with the contents of Inside Out, I left them in the alley, free for anyone to take, which seemed appropriate: curbside, with the rest of the garbage, defined Inside Out to me now.

I crawled into bed, apathetic, detached, disinterested, and indifferent to life now. I lacked the ability or ingenuity to salvage my life. I stopped fighting. Forced to concede this contentious battle, I surrendered. I gave myself permission to cease combat to cry myself to sleep.

Waking up Monday morning, I feel pulverized and relieved. Oddly relieved. For the first time in seventeen years, I didn't have to go to the office. I had no office to call my own. I had nowhere to go, nothing I had to force myself to do today. Acknowledging I had nowhere to be, I made arrangements to play volleyball. Today, tomorrow, and every day, including the largest six-man volleyball tournament. Five years had passed since I last participated in this event. I needed to be surrounded by the camaraderie of friends, some new, others I've known from my first year. No one knew what had transpired this week, or in the past months; I ensured that my failures were not exposed.

I could not let anyone know of my failures. I especially could not let anyone know of my plans, in the event of becoming homeless by month's end. No one could know. As long as I was playing volleyball, I could keep my other life separate. As long as I was smiling and cheering for our team, no one would see the pain I was in. My beach nickname was Dr. Dimples for a reason; I could not let down my guard, abandon my beach persona. It was who I was to the people I played with. Unable to keep up my charade, I left during the second match of the day. Playing volleyball no longer interested me. The sport I turned to and counted on to bring me back to life was failing me now too.

I was unable to face Mom. I stay occupied in my room. She knew, although not the entire truth of how dire the situation was.

As long as she thought I was trying to come up with a solution, she'd leave me alone.

Another week went by; no plan took shape. The third week rolled by; still no progress. I lost any desire to eat, signaling the terror I felt was too much for my mind to accept. I have completely shut down. And I no longer cared. It was all too much for me to process.

I accepted an invitation to meet a friend for lunch, one more person I needed to say goodbye to. I avoided any mention of the turn life had taken. I enjoyed listening to my friend share her life, but I wanted to go home so I could just be alone. She slipped an envelope into my hand and instructed me to open it before we parted.

"I know you are in trouble," she said. "I don't know how much trouble you're in, or what you really need to help. But I want to offer you this as a gift so you can figure it out. I know you will, and I trust that you will. I've been in trouble, and people stepped in to help me when I needed it most. I'd like to pay it forward for you now."

I opened the enveloped and stared at a check; unable to look up, I could not fully comprehend what was happening. The amount would cover five months of rent.

"I don't understand," I said. "How did you know?"

"You aren't a very good liar," she replied. "I could see you were in trouble last time I saw you. No matter how much you tried to hide behind your smile, I knew you were not okay. Whatever is going on, I hope this will help you."

"I have no words."

"No words are necessary. I believe in you. We all need a little help sometimes."

Chapter 50

Okay, God, spirit, universal intelligence: I have no words. I cannot begin to comprehend the gift you gave me.

"I know your heart is open, that you want answers. I need you to be free of worry to hear what I have to say. I know that the office has been cumbersome and the financial distress is too much, disabling you from listening with the deepest, open heart you need in order to hear, to really hear. I know you need time to process all of the events in order to go forward. So here you are, free to be with me, completely and without distractions. Get your journal and prepare to receive what your heart has been needing to hear."

I spent hours every day, sitting on my bed, writing with a fury. For four months, I downloaded and wrote, hoping to capture every insight coming through with such clarity, making no mistake of its divine nature.

The dismantling and deconstructing of my life, my choices, decisions, actions, and behaviors, every event, situation, and circumstance, lined up with unmistakable clarity. Answers were what I yearned for most. As the pieces fell into place, I figured out how the fuck I ended up there.

Every insight was written: I was empty. I was full. I was complete, and I was just beginning. In the final month of my gifted rent, a girlfriend notified me of a part-time chiropractic position up with her company, if I was interested. The exact number of hours being offered were the precise amount needed to pay rent each month.

God, spirit, universal intelligence, life force, energy had a plan. I could no longer pretend I couldn't see it. I could no longer deny the truth of what I experienced in my life now. This job was not a long-term career, but a gift for me to begin my life. I accepted with graciousness and gratitude.

For almost twenty years, I had worked with injured patients, teaching the fundamental need for time for healing from injuries, time to recover from illness. Sometimes, the mind needs to go through its own kind of physical rehabilitation therapy, as well.

Physical, mental, and emotional rehabilitative therapy was what I considered my job to be. I could use my fundamental skills while not requiring too much intellectually or creatively from me. Learning to walk again after a surgically repaired leg; that's how I felt at work. One step at a time, creating a routine, working, bringing myself back to life. A kind of work therapy was progressively making my mind stronger, getting my intellectual capacities firing again, lighting the fire within.

The internal desire to expand, grow, evolve steadily intensified; I needed to create, to use my gifts, talents, intellect, experiences, and abilities to do more. Internally, I knew what more meant for me, yet I wasn't sure I was ready. I reconnected with my inner compass; I had the discipline to get up at four o'clock in the morning. It was in the quiet stillness of the early morning where I heard the calling of my heart, without the distractions of the outside world.

I knew what I needed to do, what I had to do. It was time to go. The rumbling was loud, the calling flirting with me, daring me to say yes.

I accept, I tell my heart.

PART 5

Chapter 51

On October 1, I went to visit Mom.

"Hey, Mom," I said after entering her room. "How's it going?"

"Just okay," she replied. "My arm feels tired, heavy. I'm having a hard time holding it up."

"Let me adjust you, and hopefully with some sleep, you'll feel better in the morning."

"Can you adjust my back too? It's hurting."

"Sure."

"You feeling better, Mom?"

"No, not really. I didn't sleep very well; maybe I need some vitamins this morning."

"Sure, I'll get what you need."

"Did you sleep okay? How is your energy today?"

"I don't know what it is; I feel really tired. Maybe I'm coming down with something. I know I've been pushing myself a lot lately. I'm sure I'll be fine in a few days."

"Okay, let's just pay attention and see how you feel in a week."

"I think I need to see a doctor; it's been over a week. I feel really tired, my back hurts, and my arm feel really funny."

"Do you want me to go with you?"

"No, they'll probably just do tests; you don't need to take off work for that."

"Okay, we'll figure out a plan together once we know what's happening."

Smiling to reassure Mom I would be there to help in any way I could. I felt so uncomfortable watching her body changing. I felt helpless, powerless, and useless, as her daughter and as a doctor. Inept, doing nothing to help; nothing I did helped Mom feel better.

"It's been a month," I said. "Any new tests or results?"

"The labs and x-rays are negative. I know something is wrong. I'm having trouble walking up the stairs. I feel like I am going to fall. They're doing an MRI next."

This can't be happening, I thought. *Mom can't be getting sick or old. She's my mom. It's going to be okay.*

The spine MRIs were all negative. The doctor sent her to a neurologist. It takes two months to get an appointment.

"We cannot wait that long," I said. "You cannot walk more than a block now; something is going on, and we need to find out now. I'll call the neurologist and take you."

I put on my strong doctor face, letting Mom know I was going to take charge and get her the answers she and I both needed to hear (but we didn't really want to hear).

I liked being in doctor mode. There was a plan. There were action steps to take. There was a path: follow the algorithm of symptoms and tests, and a conclusion with treatment protocols and options will appear. I loved being in doctor mode. I got to engage my left brain, the logical, functional, rational, analytical, intellectual parts of my mind that were clear, concrete, and direct in application. The linear way of approaching life's challenge was comfortable; there was action to take, to get lost in, to disengage from the uncomfortable emotions that were surfacing.

Oh, God, this can't be. We don't have a diagnosis, but I can see the signs and symptoms and where they are pointing. Oh, God, this can't be; she's my mom.

When Mom's symptoms began to surface and the tests came back negative, I knew I was going to have to step into the fire and face all of the fears and uncomfortable feelings I had denied, suppressed, ignored, and pretended were not real. I was going to have to face every feeling, emotion, memory, event, situation, and circumstance involving Mom. Whatever feelings surfaced, I had to stand my ground, step into the ring, and do battle with whatever fear was attached that I wanted to avoid.

"Christmas is next week," I said one day. "What do you want for our special Christmas meal this year, Mom? Are you going to cook something fabulous for us?"

"No, I don't really feel like cooking anymore. It's too hard for me now."

I couldn't look at Mom as I asked. Even without a diagnosis, I suspected one of two diseases were making their way through her body. She was fragile and losing weight. Her mobility was dwindling, and she could no longer do the basic day-to-day essentials of daily living. She was dying in front of me, and there was nothing I could do. I was not ready for this. I couldn't do this. I felt this was going to be our last Christmas together. I think Mom knew too; she just didn't want to say it.

God, I can't go through this. I don't know how to do this.

I was conflicted as I carried on my day to care for Jasmine, for myself, and for Mom. Part of me wanted to be with Mom, another part wanted to run away. The force of two distinct feelings pulled me in opposite directions. I went numb to not have to choose one side over the other. I spent less and less time with Jasmine; her school needs and our mother-daughter times together were waning. Focus on work and rebuilding the business were put on the back burner for now. Both choices were necessary but caused tumultuous sensations in me. I didn't want to have to give up my life, put my world on hold.

Finally, there was news from Mom's exams: "The brain scans are all clear. Her neurologic exam shows signs of upper motor neuron weakness but nothing definitive. I want to refer her to the UCLA Neurology Department. Unfortunately, their next appointment isn't until four months from now."

"Four months? That's unacceptable. You can see she's no longer able to walk on her own; she falls if not supported. Her muscle function is deteriorating rapidly. We can't wait four more months; it's already been three months since this all started."

I yelled at the doctor on the phone; rage surfaced to levels I was both familiar and uncomfortable with. Rage made me shut down, disconnect, and want to turn off all emotional consciousness in my heart and mind. It was too much. I couldn't feel these feelings and function as a daughter and doctor at the same time.

I went through the motions to keep the day-to-day requirements for our household to function. Wildly fluctuating surges of fear overpowered any attempt to remain optimistic.

One night, I heard a thud: "Mom, are you okay? What happened?"

I screamed as I entered the room. She had fallen out of bed, onto the dog bed.

"I thought I could make it to the bathroom," she said, "then when I stepped out of bed, my legs could not hold me. I collapsed."

It's happening, I thought. *This is really happening. I am losing her. My biggest fear is becoming a reality, and I can't stop it. I don't know how I'm going to take care of her. I can't face life without her.*

"Can you take me to the emergency room?" she said softly. "I feel really tired and can't sit up. I'm having trouble breathing."

"Okay, Mom, let's go. Are you ready for this? Once you leave home, you may not be coming back."

"I know. I'm ready to go. I'm ready to meet my maker."

"Don't say that," I replied. "I am not ready."

"I know. But we need to face the truth. I'm not getting any better; the doctors can't tell me what is going on, so they don't have any way of helping me. We need to prepare; we need to get everything in order, and you need to prepare yourself and make plans for Jasmine. I know I don't have much time. I can feel it."

I sat with Mom in the ER waiting room at UCLA Hospital, holding her hand, her frail little fingers intertwined in mine. Almost twelve hours later, after they admitted her, I went back home. Even with Jasmine, the silence in the house was eerie. Mom liked to keep the radio on for the dog when she left; today, she forgot to turn it on when we left.

It was the first night in my apartment without her in the two years since she moved in. I wondered if her fall on the sidewalk was an early sign we overlooked.

So this was what our life will look like: The house was so quiet, so still without her. I wanted my apartment back, but not like this. Mom and I were uncomfortable living in such tight quarters with each other, but we made it work. Secretly hoping a neighboring studio unit would become available, I accepted a full-time position at the clinic so we could pay for our space. I knew it was time for us to have space; it was important for Jasmine to reclaim her room to express herself in. I could feel the shifting energy, suggesting the time had come for us to make a change. I was willing to make some changes; this was not one I had considered as an option. The thought of Mom dying never entered my mind. No way; she was the tough, stubborn little French lady who could bully her way through anything.

"The doctor wants to keep me for a few days to run a few more tests," she told me one day, "to confirm."

"Confirm what exactly?" I asked.

"That I have ALS," she replied. "Lou Gehrig's disease. You were right. I didn't believe you when you said it was possible. I didn't want to believe you."

"The doctor said we don't know much about this disease. It may be three weeks, three months, or three years. There weren't any options that we can reliably count on to slow the progression of this disease. They'll make sure I'm set up with what we need at home."

"Well, Mom, now we know what we're dealing with," I said. "Do you understand how this disease will progress and what to expect?"

"Yes. I know I'll continue to lose the use of my legs and arms. As the disease takes over the nerves in my brain, I'll no longer be able to walk, sit up, or move on my own. Eventually, it'll attack the muscle that controls my diaphragm, and I'll no longer be able to breathe on my own."

"Mom, I'm really scared. I don't know what to do or what to say right now."

This was the first honest statement I ever told Mom about my feelings. I never wanted to show any emotions. I learned to suppress how I felt. Until then. I couldn't hold anything back; it was too important, and we didn't have much time. We had much to do but even more to say.

As her symptoms became more pronounced, my awareness changed from "She could die" to "She will be dying soon." I yearned to have deep meaningful conversations with her about her life, our life our time together. I was afraid we wouldn't have enough time to arrive at this place I dreamed of for us. The reality hit me that she may die before we could have the kind of mother-daughter relationship I yearned for.

"What do you want to do, Mom? I will accept and support any decision you make, whatever you want."

"I want to stay home. I don't want any extra life-saving measures. You hear me? I don't want any machines keeping me alive. It's my time to meet God. I want to go be with Jesus. Don't do anything to keep me alive, okay? I just want to be home until I die."

"Okay, Mom. I promise. We'll figure this out, as we always do. It's what we do: We figure things out, how to manage, how to survive, how to make it through. We'll figure it out together. I'll talk to the nurses and get you all set up here at home, and I'll take care of you. What about your friends? Do you want to see them? Are you okay to have them come and see you? They can come while I'm at work and keep you company, keep you safe. They've been asking how they can help. Your friends want to help. They want to support you, us."

"In a few days," she said. "I need a few days to prepare myself."

"All right, you let me know when you are ready. In the meantime, I will have the home care nurses start coming."

"That's good. I feel tired; I want to take a nap now. I love you."

"I love you, too, Mom."

After hearing the diagnosis, I could see that Mom had stopped fighting. Her usual sparkling blue eyes, reflecting her love of life, had dimmed. She'd accepted that she was dying. As I watched her sleeping, I knew it would be closer to a few months than a few years. Mom would not allow herself to stay alive if she could not fully live.

Oh, God, spirit, universe, life force, energy, I need you now. How am I going to do this? How am I going to get through this?
"One feeling at a time."

Right now, my heart hurts. It hurts so much, too much for me. I can't do this.

"You can, and you will. You will because you need to, because it's the only way you know how to be and get through this. Fourteen years ago, when your father was dying, you couldn't be with him, physically or emotionally. Now you can be with your mom through this. You are not alone, although right now, you feel like you are. I know; it's just you taking care of your mom and Jasmine. This will be hard, but I will be here. Come talk to me every day, anytime. Talk to me. Let your heart break open and pour all of its contents out on me. Use your journal; write. I will guide you as you go."

At my father's funeral, I made a promise to myself to never disappear on my mom when it was time. I was unable to be present, to him, to myself, the final year of his life, and the pain haunted me.

I promised to be fully present to the experience I was in now, for the entire duration. No matter what, I would show up for myself, for Mom, and for Jasmine in the most honest and authentic way possible, no matter how ugly it looked. I promise to allow every emotion to surface, every feeling to be acknowledged, and every sound I heard. I promised to share with her feelings that were necessary, thoughts and ideas that needed to be expressed. I promised to show up every day and face the day, to the best of my ability. Not with a smile, not with a facade of strength, not with a warrior's suit of armor, but with a heavy heart that didn't know what else to do.

"One feeling at a time. One pain at a time. One fear at a time. I will not leave you. I will not abandon you. Mom, Jasmine and Tash: I can do this for all of you. You know in the coming weeks and months, there will be a lot of feelings and memories surfacing. You will need to wrestle with the past and reconcile everything now with your mom. Time is limited. You need the courage to talk, to ask, to share everything and anything with your mom. Time is urgent now; there is no later or someday. It is now. Mom is deteriorating quickly; it will be soon."

"Good morning, Mom. How are you feeling today?"
"Not so good. I am ready to see my friends now. I'm finally okay with them seeing me like this."
Well, here we go, spirit, God. Please help me help Mom. I need to work and take care of Jasmine, and I can't do this alone. You promised.

Dear God, this is too intense; my heart hurts too much. The intensity is thick; it is heavy. It is too much for me to bear. I'm afraid, afraid that the pain of longing for her for the rest of my life will suffocate me, will paralyze me.

What was happening to our family and our home was too much. I donated Mom's car and put her beloved dog to sleep in one afternoon; it was too much. It was all too much. Mom had given away her possessions and opted to help Shilo, her gentle giant malamute/shepherd furry friend, out of his misery. I was doing the best I could to keep everything under control. I couldn't feel all of this and function. I needed to shut down.

"Just stay present," the voice in my head comforted me as I wrote. "You are doing your best; you don't need to do any more than what you are."

I wanted to stay open and be present, but I couldn't. Intuitively, I knew this was the most important thing for me to do. To survive, to live through this pain, I needed to feel it, all of it, no matter how intense it got.

I found myself going through the motions. Caring for Mom's daily needs was exhausting. My poor Jasmine; her needs were pushed to the wayside. I had no idea if she was doing her homework; I had not checked any of her schoolwork in months. I asked her about it, but she knew that as much as I wanted to help her, I just couldn't.

This was temporary, I told her when we talked about what was happening. She was watching television alone on the couch; I forced back the tears and reminded myself I was doing the best I could. I was not a bad mother or a bad daughter. I could only do so much in one day; it was the best I could do, although I wished I could do more.

I sat on the edge of Mom's bed and watched her sleep. Her face looked peaceful, more calm than when she was awake. In her waking hours, she was agitated, anxious, angry, and upset. This disease was taking its toll on her. She was unable to continue her day-to-day personal routine. I did my best to keep some sense of order and dignity in her life.

Dear God, I feel so guilty. I don't want to take care of Mom any longer. I'm exhausted. I can't take care of her properly. Jasmine is falling behind in school, and it's my fault. Caring for her is taking so much out of me. I can't sleep. I go to work unable to pay attention. I only hope my lack of focus is not too noticeable. I'm doing my best to hide my distracted energy. I feel guilty that I want this to end so we can move on. What a shitty daughter I've become; what kind of person have I become? Who says these kinds of things about their own mother?

It was hard to look at Mom. I was afraid she could tell I was angry, not at her but at this disease. I was angry at this disease that I could not help her manage or control. I was angry at this disease for intruding on our lives and fucking up the status quo. I was angry that this disease had taken away Mom's will to live, her fight, her joie de vivre. I was angry this disease had left a physical body I called Mom but took the life from her. I just felt angry, angry I could not do anything but watch Mom suffer as she endured this disease. If I didn't find a way to release this rage, it would consume me. I could feel the effects already affecting me. I couldn't sleep; I tried to work out but was too weak. At work, I was unable to pay attention to patients. I hoped I didn't get fired.

I said in my mind. *I have to let her go. For my sanity, for my health, for my child's well-being.*

One by one, Mom's friends scheduled time to be with her. Every day, there was at least one visitor; most days, two or three would cram into her room, helping her eat or just sit by her bedside, listening to more of her stories about how she came to America in 1968 and what life was like in Paris just after the war, anything about her life she was willing to share. They all listened intently, as if keeping her talking would keep her alive longer, giving her reason to stay with us longer.

I could hear her voice becoming weaker; it was harder to share her life stories, taking more and more effort to talk and to swallow. She grew weaker. Sitting up in bed required too much effort, so she lay on her side. The cat nuzzled the nape of her neck.

"How are you feeling this morning, Mom? Are you hungry? I have your coffee."

This was how we started every day. Each morning, I prepared Mom's breakfast and bathed her, gathering her bedside necessities for the few hours she'd be alone: the remote, phone, Bible, and snacks to eat. Most days when I returned, however, the food was left on its plate where I left it. The chocolate and sparkling wine, however, had been consumed.

God, this disease and Mom are becoming such a fucking pain. Lifting her out of bed to the bathroom every thirty minutes was fucking ridiculous. Are you fucking kidding me? I couldn't keep up with the insatiable demands she placed on me. She had me running to every store in town to get one item of her favorite food to eat, then she didn't even eat it. What the fuck? I was sick of this. I tried to make her as comfortable as I could, but nothing worked. She complained all day about everything. I tried to have compassion and be kind, but come on. My rage monster was seething. Froth spewed from my lips with every word; it was best if I shut up and said nothing. I could not let Mom see me like this. It was not fair to either of us. ALS had all of us hostage. Mom was a prisoner in her body, and me, a slave to the demands of the disease. God, getting up at 3 a.m. to squeeze a moment of peace and quiet before the day started was wearing on me. Please keep me safe as I drive, as I work, as I live, so that I am not involved in any accidents. I am doing my best to just get through every day.

"Is there anything I can get you," I asked, "anything that you need? I'll be in and out all day today, mostly out.

I hurried to get out of the house, the energy of death and dying hanging in the air like bad exhaust from a diesel car.

"Can you come and sit with me?" Mom asked, her hand gently patting the edge of her bed. "Just come sit with me. I want to look at you. You look tired; are you doing okay? I know this is hard on you. Don't worry; it won't be for very much longer."

I collapsed onto my mom's lap, losing all composure. Gasping for air between sobs, I held onto Mom with as much force as she could handle. Maybe if I squeezed her hard enough, she would stay longer.

I'm sorry if I make you feel bad, Mom. I said to God, I don't want Mom to feel bad; this is not her fault. It's not my fault, it's nobody's fault. I'm not mad at her. I'm sorry for thinking I'd be better off without her. I'm sorry for feeling out of my mind with insane ideas that I'd somehow feel relieved if she were gone. I didn't mean to say it, I take it back.

"I see you with Jasmine," Mom told me. "You are an amazing mother, better than I ever was for you. You're so patient with her, so gentle. I was never that way with you. I see how you just hold her and let her tell you about her day. You listen to her every word; I wish I did more of that with you. You're an amazing daughter. Thank you. Thank you for taking such good care of me. You've always been my reason for living. You were my reason to stay alive. Everything I did, I did for you, for us, so you could have everything

I didn't have. I wanted to give you everything I tried, but I couldn't. And I am sorry for that."

"Mom," I said, "don't you know? You gave me the most important gift of all. You gave me what matters most, what mattered most, what I strive to give to Jasmine every day. You gave me a mom who loved me. Not a single day went by that I didn't know you loved me. You may not have liked me some of the time, but I knew with absolute certainty that you loved me. Never has a single day gone by without me knowing, in the depths of my heart, you were willing to do anything for me, for us to survive, for you to give me a better life. Don't doubt for one second I ever, ever doubted your love for me."

"You thought I didn't like you?" Mom asked. "You did things I didn't like, and you did make me mad, a lot. Why do you think I didn't like you?"

"I know you love me," I said, "but you never liked me when I was being me, when I would cry, or feel sad, or mope around the house. I always had the feeling I needed to be like you, that you liked me more when I was like you: emotionally detached, a fighter, a warrior, a survivor. My way of being was too emotional, and I thought that you hated me when I showed any emotions."

"I didn't know you felt that way," she replied. "I didn't hate your moodiness. I've always known you to be extremely sensitive. I've seen how you are with people, your friends, how much you care about them, their feelings. They matter to you; your while life, people's feelings have always mattered so much to you. I just didn't know what to do with them. Your emotions felt too big, too emotional for me to understand. It was easier for me to ignore them and let you deal with them on your own because I didn't know how to handle them. You are so good at that, at feeling your emotions. It is why your patients love you, why your friends love you, and why Jasmine loves you. She feels safe with you. You listen to her stories and her feelings. I know I never did that with you, and I'm sorry."

199

"Well, you're doing it now," I said. "Listening to me crying, sharing with you, letting me tell you how afraid I am. I am really scared, Mom. I'm scared of how life will be without you. I'm scared that I'll miss you too much to be able to function. I am scared."

"I know you are," she replied, "and I know you'll miss me, some days more than others. But you'll be able to function; you will go on. You have to; you have a beautiful little girl who needs you. When I leave, you'll paint and redecorate the room to make it hers again. You'll have your apartment back, and you'll go on. Because that is life. It is what happens. We knew this day would be coming; we just didn't know it would be now. I thought I would have another ten years or so. I wasn't planning on living with you that long, but at least near you.

"Thank you for taking such good care of me," she continued, "for doing all you do. Thank you for keeping your promise to keep me here at home with you. But now, I need you to make a new promise: I need you to promise to come see me when you can. I want to go to a nursing home. I don't want you to fuss over me anymore. I can see taking care of me is too much for you to do by yourself. I hear you at night crying; I know you're not sleeping. I can't do this to you. I want to go."

"But Mom," I said, "this time, if you go, it's permanent. You won't be coming home. I won't be able to see you every day."

"I know, and it's okay. I don't want for you to come home one day and find me dead. I don't want Jasmine to wake up and find me dead. I don't want your final memories of me to be in this room when the paramedics come to take my body. I don't want that."

"Okay, okay," I agreed. "I'll call the social worker and see what's available this week."

"Okay, good. I love you. Now stop crying and get going to work."

"What's taking the social worker so long to find a facility for me?" Mom asked the following week.

"It's only been a week, Mom. We're looking a place with hospice that's in our budget."

"I can't stay here," she protested. "You have to find a place for me. I'm scared when you're gone and I'm alone. I can't move. I get can't up. I can't speak on the phone."

"I'll call again," I said, "but it's Saturday. I'm not sure they can do anything over the weekend."

"I know you're doing your best," she said. "I just want this to be over."

I had no words to respond to Mom's desperate pleas. I could see this disease was beginning to break her down, physically, mentally, and emotionally. I heard her crying in the night, calling out to Jesus to come and take her. I knew she wanted to die; she wanted to go before she was completely incapacitated.

"It's a regular Monday for me,' I said. "I'll be at work but will be close to my phone. I'm sure the social worker will find a place for you. You have friends coming over today; you'll be safe. I'll be home later, and we'll figure it out."

"Go to work," she said. "I'll be fine."

As I left, I could see Mom's mind working overtime, coming up with a plan. She was always coming up with a plan; it was what she did, how her mind worked. She'd say, "Gotta have a plan."

Nearing the end of my shift, I hadn't heard back from the social worker yet. I was about to call on my way home but then noticed Mom was calling me.

"What's happening?" I said when I picked up.

"I am at the hospital," Mom said. "I checked myself in. They are admitting me. Can you come say good night to me?"

"Mom, what happened?"

"I was having a hard time breathing and got scared, so I called 911. I wanted to be admitted. I wanted to be here. I feel safe here.

They'll find me a home to go to. And they gave me medication so I'm not in pain."

"Okay, Mom. I'll come back tomorrow morning with some good coffee. But if you see Jesus in the night, it's okay to go. If he calls you, go ahead and go. I know it's what you want. Jasmine and I, we'll be okay."

The next morning, I arrived at her room.

"Hi, Mom, you're awake? I have coffee for you."

"I guess Jesus didn't come yet," she said. "I know he will soon.

"The nurses tell me they have a facility to transfer you to. You'll be there tonight."

"That's good news," she said. "I'm really tired. I'm going to go to sleep now. Can you bring Jasmine to see me later?"

"Yes, we'll be here. Get some rest. And remember, if you see Jesus, it's okay to go to him. Jasmine and I, we'll be okay."

I hugged Mom in her hospital gown, with tubes attached. I left, unsure if I'd see her alive again. "I love you, Mom."

"I love you, too. Thank you for being my daughter, for taking such good care of me. I'll keep taking care of you from above. I'll be with you; don't worry."

It was 10:30 p.m.; I knew I needed to sleep, but I couldn't. Mom was being transferred to her new home. She was heavily medicated and sleeping. She had her phone; I knew she'd call me if she woke up before visiting hours. I must have had some sleep; my phone woke me. It was Mom.

"Come get me," she said. "You need to come get me. Please get me out of here; they hurt me. Please hurry; don't leave me here another night."

Her haunting voice echoed in my bones.

"What happened, Mom?" I asked.

"I don't know. They left me in bed all night, and strange people kept coming in and talking to me, but I couldn't speak. I couldn't move. Please don't leave me here."

"I'm on my way," I said. "I'll be there in about thirty minutes."

When I got to the nursing home, I spoke to the supervisor.

"Your mom is on heavy narcotics," he explained. "The pain and other medications are affecting her. She was crying out for her mom through the night. She woke up and didn't know where she was."

I went into Mom's room.

"Where were you?" she asked. "I called you yesterday. Why didn't you come for me? How long do I have to stay here?"

"Mom, did anyone hurt you?" I asked.

"I was crying all night," she said sadly. "No one came when I called. They left me alone all night. I was calling you, but you didn't answer. I'm sorry. The medication is making my head fuzzy. I didn't know what happened to me. I didn't know where you were."

Once I felt confident Mom was safe, that she was not in harm's way, I sat with her on the bed, helping her drink the coffee I brought for her. It had only been six weeks since receiving the diagnosis; she was deteriorating rapidly. Already close to 75 percent of her muscle functions were gone. I was prepared. I expected I would be getting *that* phone call any day. Until then, her friends still wanted to be by her side, keeping her company while I worked. I kept her visiting schedule full. Although the medications helped her stay pain free, they altered her mental capacity, but at least she was comfortable. That was my promise to her: to keep her safe and comfortable. It was all I had to give her now.

I thought I was doing a good job of handling the emotions as they arose. Seeing my mom in the nursing care facility, medicated and so fragile; the final chink in the dam came crashing down. The remaining contents lodged in my heart, gushing out. This five-year-old little girl was no longer able to keep it together; she unleashed a tantrum on the facility administrator, the staff, and any patient able to hear.

"No, no, no. We can't leave her here. We're not supposed to leave her here. We promised to keep her at home. We promised to take care of her until the end. We promised to keep her until we were ready to let her go."

My forty-something-year-old body containing the terrified five-year-old started jumping up and down, stomping her feet on the floor, pounding her fists on the wall. No, we couldn't leave her there. This could not be where she died. She was not supposed to die now. She could not die. We had too much to talk about still. We still had too much to do. We were supposed to go to France to see Jasmine launch her fashion designs. We were supposed to celebrate her eightieth and ninetieth birthdays together. She was supposed to see more sunsets and cook more crepes. She was supposed to teach French to more people, to share more stories about France after the war and coming to America. She was not supposed to die now, not like this. My little girl self collapsed on the tile floor of the visiting room floor, crumbled into the fetal position, and refused to move.

All of my hopes and dreams, our plans, came crashing at once, short-circuiting my mind. I couldn't leave her. She was my mom. I couldn't let her go; I didn't want to let her go. There was so much more life we were supposed to have together. This couldn't be how it ended.

After almost an hour on the floor, alternating episodes of uncontrollable sobbing and yelling, my little girl self got up off the floor. Together, we went back into Mom's room, kissed her sleeping forehead goodbye, and promised to come back tomorrow.

My little girl self had finally made herself known, letting her terrified self come out to be heard, to be consoled, to take part in the process of letting Mom go. She let me know she had more to say, more she needed to say to me and to Mom before she died. I took her in my heart and promised to let her say whatever she needed to say, once we were in the safe and comforting space of our home.

Chapter 52

As ALS ravaged Mom's body, rendering her less able to move, I was more aware that her level of anxiety was rising. Truthfully, I was not sure if the levels of fear and anxiety were increasing or if they were becoming increasingly noticeable as ALS took away her lifestyle, her way of hiding, her means of running away, effectively disconnecting, hiding, suppressing her uncomfortable feelings, fears, and anxieties she always had.

Mom lost her ability to control anxiety when she lost control of her body, leaving her unable to move, to run away, or to work to disconnect, disassociate from the discomforts of anxiety and dis-ease in her mind.

Even as a young child, I could feel the ripples of anxiety in Mom, although I had no way to articulate the sensations I felt. I didn't know what I was feeling, the energy vibrations I was picking up on. I just knew she was upset, uncomfortable, irritated, and at times irrational (my teenage perception of her). I know I felt rebellious against her when she would incorporate me into her seemingly useless activities. I wanted no part in what I perceived as messy, out-of-balance activities, without purpose, or just a waste of time, especially anything that I perceived lacked organizational skills. That's when I cast my disapproving critical judgments on her, angry that I had to alter my plans to accommodate her lack of planning. I was angry that she recruited me to participate in her ceaseless activities; only now do I understand they were Mom's way of coping, distracting herself from the incessant chatter in her mind.

What I could not see then, or really understand until the illness forced Mom to be still, was the anxiety and fear that constantly circulated in her mind.

Mom offered some of her childhood experiences with me. Piecing together stories of her past, with stories of my grandmother, along with my memories of our life with my father, a picture was coming into focus. As she began to share her fears with me, the terror that I felt was surfacing. I carried the deepest terror as a secret my entire life, a secret that has unconsciously been operating in my mind; only now, as I pull the thread, the fears and terrors are beginning to unravel the terrors that held Mom and I prisoners together.

I carried a secret shame my entire life, about being born biracial. I was riddled with confusion, humiliation, guilt, and disgust, believing it necessary to keep quiet about these horrific feelings of contempt I felt about my parents and their decision to give birth to me.

What I could not hear in the passing voices, what I could not understand in the stares, I understood in feelings: disgust and contempt. Feelings that penetrated my skin from people; some strangers, some not. Some authority figures, some not. The look of disgust when my mother introduced me as her daughter. The same energy echoing in me as a young child when people would ask, "What are you?" Not who was I, or what was my name, but "What are you?" as if whatever I answered was supposed to justify how I looked.

Because how I looked was unacceptable to them. My mocha brown skin, not quite black, definitely not white, a perfect mixture, a fifty-fifty blend of both, not welcomed.

I received the same messaging at school when filling out standardized tests asking for race. The options were black, white,

Hispanic, and Asian (in later years, "other" was an option). I could only choose one. I felt I would dishonor my dad for checking white and betray my mom for checking black. I opted to leave that question blank; not to make a statement, I just didn't know how to answer the question, further penalizing me for leaving a question unanswered.

Growing up, I believed I was bad, inherently wrong for the color of my skin. I was not white or black, but a diluted version of both; I didn't fit in to any group, any category. I was different. I was mixed, and society told me and my mother that her heinous atrocity of coming to this country, a foreigner not understanding the rules of race, marrying and having a child with a black man, that her stupidity destined us both for a life of pain and misery.

Unconsciously, these messages from the world made me believe I was inherently worthless for the choices my parents made in having me when the rules said they should not have. They broke the rules, and I was the guilty, shameful outcome of their union. Television told me my kind was inexcusable. As an other, I might be tolerated, certainly not accepted, approved of, or welcomed. Not until little Olivia appeared on TV did I ever believe someone like me would be accepted in the regular world.

The father of my childhood friend would tell me to "wash the black off my skin" if I wanted to come inside. The way he looked at me struck me with fear.

But the worst pain, the most terrifying, were the comments made to me and Mom, from as young as I could recall, from people saying I should be taken away, that Mom should not be able to keep me, that the world would be better if it could get rid of me. I slept in Mom's bed every night until high school due to the terrifying belief that someone would come and take me away. As much as Mom hovered and kept me too close at times, I understood her terror that someone would actually make real their threats to take me away.

In the dark of night, as Mom held me, she made me promise to always make sure to work twice as hard, do twice as much work, to prepare twice as much to look twice as perfect. Whatever I did, I needed to do twice the requirement, twice the effort. Not to stand out, but to blend in. My safety was determined by my ability to blend in, to be as equal as possible, to not draw attention to me so I could stay safe and protected. To me, her advice made sense; I believed her. This was how I was to protect myself from the big, mean world of people who would be looking to harm me, not for doing anything wrong, but for the wrongness of my skin.

When I was five, six, ten, twelve, eighteen, and twenty, the message was the same. People in the world were out to hurt us, to intentionally cause ill will to us, for her "sins and mistakes" of birthing me. Although Mom was never sorry for having me, before her death, she told me she was sorry that I had to face the challenges I did because of her choice to marry my father. She was sorry for being so naive and not knowing how different America was from France about race.

The deep-seated unconscious belief in my mind was that the best I could hope for in my life was for people to tolerate me. If people liked me, that was a bonus. While being liked was not my goal, being tolerated was. Because to be tolerated meant I was safe, safe from the intentional, malicious harm others may want to cause me.

The terror that haunted me was that the other people who wanted to harm me were indistinguishable from those who didn't. I had no way of telling the intentions of another human being, so I had to make the decision to assume that every person had ill intentions, until proven otherwise. Even then, they could prove otherwise, but their family or friends or colleagues may not have the same ways of being; no one could be trusted. I had to fear everyone.

My goal was to be invisible or else do whatever it took to be tolerated. My survival depended on my ability to judge and discern. This was made easier if I was secretive and kept a slight coldness, aloofness, and distance from everyone. Better to keep my happy face on than to show any emotional vulnerability that someone could use against me. I was fully committed to Mom's motto, "Be like a duck."

In the loving space of our home, with uninterrupted time and attention, I gave my little girl self the privacy and dignity to say, to write, to share whatever was on her mind, whatever was in her heart. She had a voice, she had feelings, and she needed to be heard, be loved, be told, unconditionally, that whatever she was feeling mattered, at least to me.

What I was feeling was angry, a rage with a kind of voracity and ferociousness that was new to me. This time, I felt angry at Mom.

I was angry that she had become so demanding, too demanding for me to fulfill her unending requests. Angry that I was unable to keep up with her relentless demands; she needed to be comfortable, to feel at peace, none of which seemed to help. I was angry that she needed more from me than I could give. I was angry that I felt like a shitty daughter for leaving Mom in a hospice facility and not being able to care for her at home.

I was scared that Mom's demands would be too much for the caregivers. If they were too much for me, I didn't know how they'd react to her constant, ever escalating demands. I was afraid they'd harm her in retribution if pushed over the edge or neglect her from exhaustion. I was angry that Mom put me in this position, now having to worry about nurses and staff and her well-being.

While I was not happy she was gone, I was happy the ordeal was over. Her physical demands had become too much, beyond what was humanly capable of me to fulfill. And I was angry with her for asking me to take on her emotional needs and make them go away for her, to ease her emotional discomfort.

But the truth was, I could not now, not ever, make her emotional pains go away. It was never my job to do so, although I accepted this role as my own as a little girl. I took on the role as her protector, her provider of comfort, but those were not my jobs to take.

I accepted this job as a little girl, from the first time I noticed that in the midst of Dad's violent rage outbursts, he would not hit her when I was in the room. I was able to protect her. Being in the room, being next to Mom, was my way of offering her protection. The problem was, I never relinquished my role as protector. My whole life, each and every decision I needed to make, I would consult my little girl self to see which option would be best for Mom, which option would best protect Mom. Although she didn't ask me directly, I accepted her safety as approval, diligently continuing my duties until the day she died.

I believed, that as her daughter, my worth was dependent on my ability to protect her, to provide her with comfort and safety. Not because she asked me to, but because as a five-year-old little girl, this was what I interpreted. I had no other way to protect her from Dad's violent behaviors. In my mind, I had to become her protector. She was all I had in this world. After Darnel left and Grandmommy died, she was all I had left. If something happened to her, I'd be left alone in a big world that looked at me with shame and disgrace for being biracial. And without her to help me grow up, the mean world could have maliciously sought to harm me. Not just hurt, but to harm, to cause mayhem and torture, as revenge for what white society perceived me to be: a stain on its pristine view of its culture.

My entire life, I carried the heavy burden that it was my job to make sure she felt peace of mind, that I could hold at bay the fears and anxieties she felt about Dad. I arrived with the shame of being unable to comfort her; she lived her life in fear. I felt the burden, the anger of having to be responsible for her. I was angry that I felt imprisoned by her fears and insecurities, that I had to ease her pain. I didn't want to. I made choices she wanted me to make to ease her fears; I felt disdain, hatred, and contempt that I dishonored and betrayed my own desires in order to do so.

"Mom," I journaled, "I chose the college you wanted me to attend, instead of the one my heart felt called to, in order to stay close to you, close to home and for you to not feel uncomfortable. I hated you for this. And I was unable to live with the hatred I felt, so I suppressed it, covered it up with food, alcohol, and work. As long as I had one of the three, I could keep the destructive forces of anger tucked away. And with a smile plastered on my face, no one was the wiser. No one knew what I really felt. I kept my feelings from you, Mom, from the world, but worst of all, I kept my true feelings from myself.

"Feelings of betrayal, compounded by the disgust of who I had become, made the levels of shame rise to unprecedented levels. Energy that needed to escape, a release, which was why the behaviors of bulimia manifested. Of course, at that time, I had no idea.

"I was angry with you, Mom, angry that I felt the burden of taking care of you alone, angry that you gave me the responsibility. I never understood why I had to be your everything, instead of being free to be me. I needed to be whoever you needed and wanted me to be for you. I was angry that you chose to live your life alone, making me shoulder the immense responsibility of caring for your needs.

"Whatever needs you felt would keep you from feeling discomfort, fear, anxiety, I had to alter any of my plans, my ideas, my life, to preemptively figure out your unconscious fears and tailor my life plans accordingly. I was angry at feeling such a loss of control in my life. Bulimia gave me something I could control, that you could not change or interfere with. Secretly, I took pleasure in seeing you upset about my addiction; you were powerless to control it or me.

"But most of all, when Grandmommy died and you sent me to Europe for the summer, I hated you. I didn't understand. I didn't know you were overwhelmed by the emotions of your mother's death and my father's threats. I didn't know you sent me away because you thought I'd have more fun with them than with you. I didn't know because you didn't tell me.

"So I assumed you were tired of me, tired of having to take care of me. I hated you for sending me away in the time of my greatest need. I needed you then more than any other time in my life. I felt abandoned and believed that you were tired of my emotional outbursts, of my crying, of my moods. I believed you hated me, and sending me away was just an easy way to not have to deal with me.

"That summer, I misinterpreted your actions to mean you didn't really like me, that although you loved me, I annoyed you. I was not like you, making me burdensome to you. That summer, I unconsciously made the decision to always be the best helper to you, the best provider I could be for you, the best worker I could be for you, so you'd want to keep me with you. You were all I had by then. You were it, and without you, you choosing to leave me, I assumed you would be willing to get rid of me at any chance if I didn't behave accordingly, the way you wanted me to behave.

"That summer, I learned to suppress all my natural tendencies and desires in lieu of yours. I squelched my dreams and traded them for yours. I believed the more I could make myself resemble you and look less like me, you would like me more, and love me more. The more I could be like you, the less likely you were to send me away again, the less hassle I was for you.

"I believed that somehow, I could just take away your emotional pain, I could make your worries disappear. If I had the power to keep you physically safe, then I should also protect you emotionally. In your focus on taking care of our physical needs with work, you dumped your emotional issues on me. In my naivety and youth, I accepted this job as my duty and responsibility. Most of all, my worth, my purpose, and the meaning for my life were based on how well I cared for you, protected you, and provided for you. My failure to do so meant I was useless and worthless. This was the misinterpretation I unconsciously carried about myself, becoming the contract I was upholding.

"Then one day, as I finally felt the strength to share this with you, Mom, you let me know it was never my job, never my responsibility, never my purpose to care for you. And I was able to let go, able to free myself from the pact I felt bound by. I could finally let down the burden of trying to see what anxieties my life's choices could bring My mom in order to choose accordingly. I did not now or ever need to fix Mom or take away her pain. Making her discomforts tolerable in order to keep her from abandoning me, physically or emotionally, was no longer my job, but in truth, it never was my job to do so.

"Somewhere along the way," this journal entry concluded, "a little girl bought into the misbelief that if she became her mom's provider, her mom's protector, the person who could relieve her mom of all the emotional and physical discomforts that ailed her, that she would have a purpose, a meaning, be needed, be loved, and never again be sent away."

But now, she was comfortable. Narcotics for pain and other medications soothed her; she was able to finally sleep through the night. At Mom's request, I altered her visiting schedule to accommodate just one person per day, each afternoon, when she had the most energy to engage. Still, not a day went by that Mom was alone; every day, she had a friend come sit by her side, keep her company, bring her chocolates, and hold her hand while I worked. I knew our time was coming to an end. The phone was always by my side, expecting a call any moment.

"I brought pictures of Jasmine's room, like you asked," I said one day. "I painted her room and the entire apartment. We have new furniture; just waiting on the bed she wants, and we'll have it all done."

"It looks really nice," Mom said. "Jasmine, do you like your new room?"

"Yes, Grandmommy," my daughter said. "Look at the catalogue of things I want to buy: a mirror, a sewing machine. I'll make you a pretty dress, Grandmommy. You can wear it when you see Jesus."

This was our family day. All Saturday and Sunday, we ate together and shared with Mom what projects we were working on.

"Make sure you write your book," Mom said. "It is important. Promise me you will finish you book. Jasmine needs to know your story. I wish I would have told you mine. I think it would have helped you understand me better. I am sorry I didn't."

And there it was. Mom said what I had not been able to fully articulate to myself, the deep fear I was feeling yet couldn't pinpoint.

The most difficult, most painful fear was the reality that I didn't really know Mom. I knew facts about her life, but I didn't know her emotionally Who she was, was a secret to me. Her heart, her dreams, her desires, her regrets, and her fears: I didn't know of them. I was aware of some of her fears, her wishes for me, based on pieces of stories she'd volunteer with me. Mostly, Mom was a secret to me. The reality that she was dying and that she could die without me knowing her, really knowing her, was the greatest fear I had to face about her death.

What I wanted most from Mom was a heart-to-heart, deep, mother-daughter kind of relationship, the honest expression of who we are with one another. I longed to experience Mom as the person she was, not just as the worker she was.

After she was transferred to a facility and the narcotics began to take her, I realized she was leaving; she was often already mentally gone when I came to visit. My opportunities to sit and listen to her were fading. Little by little, she was deteriorating physically and mentally. I had to make peace with the notion that we would never have the relationship I longed for us to have, the fantasy one I wished we could have.

Finally, I had to accept that Mom would most likely die without me really knowing her, all of her, the real authentic woman I knew she was, the woman in her heart she refused to let me see, acknowledge, or be privy to.

"My beautiful baby girl," Mom said; her barely audible voice had clarity, letting me know she was present and consciously in the moment. "You did good, baby. Take care of your baby, now, the way I took care of you. She needs you. You don't need to worry about me anymore. I'll be with Jesus soon."

"It's okay, Mom. We still have time. I'll be back tomorrow to hear more."

"Okay, love. See you tomorrow. Can you bring Jasmine? Can you buy her a new Easter dress and have her dance and twirl for me?"

"I will, Mom." I didn't have the heart to tell her Easter was three weeks ago.

Makeup on, off to work, then to see Mom before Jasmine's swim practice; today's schedule: a regular normal Monday.

The phone rang.

"There's been a change in your mother's condition," the administrator said gently. "You may want to come now. The hospice nurse is already here."

"Is she still alive?" I asked.

"Yes, but she's been unconscious all morning."

"Hold on, Mommy," I cried. "I'm coming. I'll be there in thirty minutes. I am on my way; wait for me."

"Mom?" I said gently, walking into her room.

She turned her head in the direction of my voice.

"She hasn't shown any signs on consciousness until now," the nurse said. "You must be her daughter. She hasn't woken up, but hearing your voice, she is with us. She can hear you."

I took off my shoes, crawled into the bed, and gathered her frail body in my arms.

"Mommy, I am here," I said. "I know you can hear me. If you can say anything, I am listening. If not, it's okay. I am here now. I am with you. I got you. You are not alone. I know you can see Jesus's face. I will hold on to you while you run to him. It's okay.

I won't hold you too tight; you can go. I will hold you until you reach his arms. I love you, and it is okay to go. Can you still hear me, Mommy? I see your eyes moving; I think you can. Before you go, I have one last thing I need to tell you; this is very important, so stay with me.

"You are and were the most amazing mommy I could have had. You were the greatest mommy, the only one I ever wanted; that's why I chose you. Before I was conceived, I asked God to give me to you because I knew you would be the perfect mom for me, the exact mom I would want and need to bring me into this world and give me everything I'd need to be alive, to survive, and to thrive. Because of you, I get to be here now. Thank you for giving me my life. Not a day passed that I didn't know, in the deepest crevices of my heart, that you loved me unconditionally. I am lucky; not every child gets to say that about their mom. Every day for the rest of my life, I can live knowing you loved me and that you will continue to love me. Wherever my journey takes me, you are with me.

"Before you leave, I need you to know: You mattered to me. You mattered to everyone you encountered. Your life mattered. All of your gifts and talents mattered. You are loved, and you matter. I know you know this because you told me before you came to the facility. You told me how amazed you were at how people kept showing up to see you, even when you were not at your best. Your appearance didn't matter; people came to see you because they love you.

"Remember before you arrived here? You told me you didn't know you were so loved. Remember? We talked about how even though this disease was taking your life now, it also gave you a gift. Remember, that although you can't say you are happy about this disease, you can feel some gratitude that you were able to experience so many of your friends coming to be with you, that you were alive to hear visitors tell you how much you mattered to them, how much you meant to hem, how much they love you, and how much you loved them. Remember? I do.

"So as you leave your body now, Mom, take with you the love and kindness and compassion of every person who loves you, prayed for you, for us, for all the people who stepped up to help me, help you. I needed so much help, and people offered, and they gave.

"I know you are waiting for me to leave so that you can leave. I am ready, but I don't want to leave just yet. I'll stay all day, until I need to pick up Jasmine. I know you don't want her last memory of you to be in dying, so I won't come back. I'll hold Jasmine in my arms tonight, as we lay in bed. If you are still here tomorrow morning, I will come. The nurse will be by your bed the entire night. If Jesus comes while I am gone, it is okay to go. I love you more than I will ever be able to tell you."

At 6:30 a.m., Tuesday, April 24, Jesus came to take my mom. She was finally free of her ailing physical body and able to swirl in the cosmos, to see the galaxies, to touch the vast blue sky. The piece of sky that beckoned her to leave France as young girl, to see beyond the gray buildings of Paris. "You are free, Mom."

The first day and night in my apartment, the silence wrapped Mom and me together. In the cocoon of the day, Mom kept her promise to look after me.

"Go be free, have fun, you are done. You have completed your contract with me. In my death, I have taken with me all of my fears and anxieties. You no longer need to carry them for me or continue them as your own. Let me take your fears from you now. Let me do for you, now, what I couldn't do for you while I was alive."

I took out my journal. I knew what I needed to let go of. I knew exactly what fears Mom was asking me to relinquish to her, the secret we had both kept. Not from one another, but together. Our shared secrets, our fears, our terrors.

PART 6

Chapter 53

Following Mom's death, I continued to have conversations with her that were too hard to have while she was alive.

If I was ever going to have the relationship with her I wanted, I needed to have those conversations with her in my head and heart. The conversations I wished for us to have, I relegated to having them in the quiet stillness of the early morning hours with my journal. I needed to have conversations with her, without her physical presence, just her spirit.

And so I did. I had all the conversations I wished I could have with her. I had them in my heart and on paper, knowing her spirit could hear me and somehow would find a way to answer me, in a way that the message could be heard by me.

I had to trust in sharing from the heart, my heart to hers, with the intention to be honestly share, for both of us. I had to trust that no matter what I said, no matter what information, feelings, thoughts, ideas came forward, I could share without judgments or criticism. Honestly sharing the most authentic version of me with Mom was going to be okay, no matter how painful or uncomfortable what I had to say felt.

One at a time, feelings surfaced. I acknowledged them as they showed up, regardless of how daunting or negatively charged they felt. One by one, the process of dismantling and deconstructing the life I had with Mom took its course. One by one, as the feelings emerged and I shared them with her, I realized I was finally experiencing the kind of mother-daughter relationship I yearned for my whole life. Although it was not how I had imagined our relationship to be, I accepted this was going to be the closest version to what I wanted and needed. This was the form of our relationship I had to accept, without wishing it was any different.

In the stillness at three and four o'clock in the morning, she wakens me. It's the time that Mom knows she'll have my complete, undivided attention to speak with me.

"I know this was hard on you," she said. "Having to care for me all by yourself, carry the entire responsibility of me on your shoulders. You had to do all of it, and you did. And I thank you. I know I was very demanding and difficult. But you cared for me anyway, the best way you knew how. You did a great job and made sure I was safe, was comfortable, and could die with dignity. You've always taken care of me, more than any daughter should have to take care of her mother, but you did it because I had no one else. I didn't have any family here. I didn't trust anyone to let them into my life after your father. I'm sorry you were alone in having to take care of me. I know you sacrificed part of your life for me. Now you are free. I want you to go and live your life the way you want to. Take Jasmine and be free. Go, do all the things you want to do before it's too late. Go, have fun."

For her celebration of life service, it was important for me to be able to speak with an open heart, a heart without any remaining unresolved issues between us. I needed to complete my work in letting go of all misinterpretations that would interfere with my ability to hold Mom in the loving space of my heart. None of her physical human issues mattered. None of our earthly disagreements mattered.

But they do matter if I hold on to them. For me to feel Mom's love, guidance, and support in my heart, my heart needed to be clear, free from any unresolved issues I was still holding onto. There were still conversations needing to be expressed and given voice. Still some heart-to-hearts that needed to be engaged in. Knowing that the only way out of the pain of Mom's death was through it, I promised myself that I would go into the abyss, the deepest crevices of my heart and mind to heal the fractures, mend the wounds, and release the negatively charged residuals of any trauma relating to her. Now, without Mom's humanness interfering, we could freely talk; without the humanness and human mess, I could finally heal.

I know Mom is always with me, always connected to me. Life is forever different now, without her physical presence in my world. Each day, my heart feels sadness and grief at the loss of her physical self, along with the joy and excitement that her spirit self will remain with me. I know I did the best I knew how to do. I continue to do the best I know how to do each day. The best I am able to offer, in any exact moment in time, is all I can offer, my best offering in that moment.

Mom still speaks to me, as if giving me the answers I need to hear from her; the 3 a.m. conversations continue.

Chapter 54

I felt an inner rage against Mom my entire life due to her anxiety and fears. Ultimately, her fears were my fears. I inherited them and expanded them. The rage was in me, carrying the misbelief that my fears were real, that I was worthless, undeserving of being safe in the world.

Until Mom's death, my life's choices and every decision I made was heavily influence by her. In my unconscious mind, I believed that my worth was based on my ability to care for her needs, putting her needs above my own at all times. I needed to protect her and keep her safe, physically and emotionally. Every choice I made in my life, I had to consider Mom's feelings and reactions. Any choice that would make her feel anxious, nervous, afraid, or in any way uncomfortable, I opted out of in order to keep her safe. Taking care of Mom instead of myself became my measurement. The choices I made were directly proportional to the amount of discomfort she was able to tolerate, how much discomfort she could live with. I had to know her discomforts, her needs, and stay within the confines of her ability to feel comfortable.

Another unconscious belief that had been wreaking havoc was the deep need to feel safe in a world that I learned to not trust, a world I believed to be evil, a world where I believed most people wanted to harm me, consciously, maliciously, and intentionally harm me because of the color of my skin. Not just the blackness of my skin, but with even more hatred for being of mixed race. My biracial background put me in harm's way by both white and black people who hated my parents for going outside of their race and comingling together. My biracial roots were such a disgrace to a society that seemed to want to keep races separated. How would I have learned different? Mom came from France, where black and white people lived among one another, in a way that was normal and accepted. It didn't occur to her just how divided the racial gap was, even in San Francisco. She was unaware of the significant times she found herself in the States. There were very few images that highlighted mixed races, let alone showcased them and showered them with love, kindness, and acceptance. My experience about my mixed race was degradation and disdain at the audacity of my parents to marry in 1969 and then produce a child from that abomination of a marriage.

Most of the choices I made were rooted in the unconscious belief that I had to pick one side over the other, choosing to hide as much of my blackness as I could in order to be liked. Not as much liked as tolerated. I believed that if I could blend in, I would be tolerated. And if I were tolerated, I would not be harmed.

As a young child, I was repeatedly told I should be taken away from my mom, as a punishment to her for her and my father's decision to marry and produce a mixed-race child. When I was a young child, adults and people in positions of authority routine scolded Mom for parading around with her "half-breed." Authorities that told us that given the chance, they would see to it that I was taken from her. I believed them, and Mom believed them; why wouldn't we? It was just us; there was no way for us to know any different. Not then, in the 1970s. That was the culture and the times we lived in then (although so much of what is happening now is recalling all my childhood fears).

The painful process of deconstructing my life continued, dismantling the beliefs that had been the rocky foundation I built an unstable life upon. The false illusions and beliefs I once thought were real were not. And as the time came for me to expand, evolve, grow, I had to let go of the beliefs that were limiting me, that had served me this far in my life, but would not support me in the direction I wanted to go.

In order to live the life I wanted, I needed to allow my vulnerable, softer side to show. I needed to find the confidence and courage to expose the raw, real me, the me that was human. My humanness, my human mess, were all a part of life, my life. I gave myself permission to live the version of me that was honest, without the need to cover my human self up; the parts of me that are sensitive, moody, and emotionally charged no longer needed to fear being harmed.

"Well, Mom, it's been ten days since you've left earth," I journaled. "I know you've been enjoying your freedom, traveling through the galaxies, sharing your heart with me, as I open mine to you. Today, the mortuary called; your body is going into the crematory today. I opted to not see you, although they said the UCLA organ recovery team did a great job after taking your brain and spine for ALS research. Your final requests are being honored. Your friends and mine continue to support Jasmine and me, but of course, you already know this. In preparing for your service, I just wanted to say I'm sorry.

"Sorry that I could not afford a better place for you, your final weeks alive. Sorry that somewhere along the way of being a doctor, I didn't know how to take care of the finances to ensure a better quality end of life for you."

Oh, my baby, you don't need to be sorry. I know you did the best you could, that we could. You once asked God to answer your question, How the fuck did you end up here? Well, here is the information to answer that question; you need to know this now: As my body goes into the flames, I can take your pain away for you. Let the final pieces of your burdened heart be set free as my body burns to ashes. Place your fears, your past, your insecurities in the box with me. I will take them from you. Once the flames take me, they will take your past with it. You no longer need to carry with you the emotional charge, the terrors you felt. The rest of your life, you will be untethered.

At Mom's urging, I reached to my journal again to write one final letter, the last remaining piece of my past that I had not yet been able to detangle myself from. With clarity and love, I unchained my emotional body from the remnants of guilt, shame, and humiliation that still pierced my heart.

Chapter 55

Dear Inside Out Wellness Center,

When we first met, I was instantly enamored with you. From our very first meeting, I said yes to you, promising to make us work, to give you whatever you needed. Your mystique lured me in with the promise of creating a better life, a future, something more grand than the dreams I imagined. I wanted to experience all you promised to give. Your grandness, your image, your energy lured me in. Your way of being intrigued me. I wanted to calibrate myself to you. I was fused with your grandiose vow of fulfilling all of my dreams, those I knew of and those not yet conscious to me.

You were difficult from the start; owning and operating a business was something I had never done. I had watched Mom tend to her own business and saw the hours, the commitment, the behind-the-scenes work necessary. I was under no illusions of your requirements. Still, I wanted you. I wanted to know you, know everything about you, what made you expand and grow, what made you recoil and retract. I dedicated myself to learning all of your traits and characteristics, suspending all judgments about you. Because most of all, I wanted our partnership to work. I had so much riding this, you and me together, my hopes and dreams of our future. Your unknown intentions were yet to be discovered, mysteries to be uncovered, our journey together yet to unfold.

My authentic love of the chiropractic philosophy, for the profession that chose me, instantly connected us. My heart's desire was always to be of service, to use my education and gifts, dedicating myself to the true meaning of *doctor*, which means "teacher." I took my oath with that intention: to teach others and care for their well-being. My love for the people I served connected me with my own heart. It was my love, in its purest form.

Early on in our relationship, you let me know of your temperament, your fickleness, making me aware of every action I made by responding, both my decisions that pleased you and those you disagreed with, from choices of staffing personnel to office hours to the ways I went about introducing you to the public through marketing. Your delicate way of being left no room for me; your instability ensured I behaved in a way you decided was best for you, regardless of my needs. In my naivety, without question or regard for my own sense of direction, I accepted your feedback as a personal indictment of my knowledge of you. I took responsibility for every fluctuation, every ripple in your efficacy. When you mirrored to me your displeasure of my actions and behaviors, I conformed, complied, and attuned myself to you.

I stayed because I wanted to. I committed to you and wanted to uphold my contract to you, to myself. I wanted to prove to myself I, too, could be a successful business owner. My youthful exuberance overlooked the unseen undercurrent of you as you reflected every mistake of the learning curve, magnifying every amateur instinct. Yet I remained your faithful student, with the belief that someday we would get along, that I would learn how to act according to your tenets: criterion you made me aware of through errors after the fact.

Within a few months, I began to experience gifts from you. Benefits began to surface that I didn't know I wanted, that I didn't know I needed. I appreciated your approval of me, your delight in my right doing efforts. As you compensated me more, my desire for

229

more also grew. Insidiously, I allowed you to make your way into my personal life. With innocuous extra hours and weekend changes of plans, you began to infringe on the rest of my life, taking more of me for your needs.

But as long as you were providing for my needs, I didn't give voice to the churning below the surface of my smile. I willingly gave a few extra hours, an extra weekend, in exchange for your accolades. Your bountiful dividends rendered me blind to the far reach of your tentacles into every area of my life.

Surreptitiously, our relationship began to change. You were changing, your needs growing more and more insatiable. I was morphing to keep up with you, assuming I was the culprit who needed to change. Growing inside of me were feelings of discontent. Feelings of hatred for you brewed as you began to consume me and my life. Resentment grew as I needed more and more energy to keep you alive and operational.

As your weight began to suffocate me, I accustomed myself to smaller and smaller breaths of air. Denying my own need for oxygen, in lieu of yours, I suppressed the loathsome feelings that were creeping to the surface. I wanted to run away. I wanted to give you up. I wanted to stop our relationship, but I couldn't.

Because by now, I am getting from you what I unconsciously wanted. What I really wanted from you, you were giving me. Far beyond financial rewards, I didn't want to relinquish you. At any cost, I made up my mind to keep you. I needed you. You gave me protection. You became my asylum. What you offered me, I was willing to sacrifice all that mattered to keep you.

Security, immunity, a safe haven. You were my shield, my coat of armor that once donned, I felt your power.

When my father was dying, you were my solace. You gifted me with a place to hide, a place to go to, with a plan I could operate on auto pilot. You took me in; you kept me distracted from all of the uncomfortable, painful feelings surfacing that I didn't want to face, that I couldn't face. I could suppress them with you. As long as you had work for me to complete, I didn't have to feel anything. I could stay numb about my feelings about my marriage, about my father, about the circumstance of my life I wanted to omit. In your arms, I never had to face any part of my life I didn't like. I could run to you and hide in you; you were there for me.

In taking care of patients, I felt like I could make up for the way I believed I mistreated my father. That somehow, if I cared for patients enough, instead of my own needs, that I could make up for not caring enough for my father when he needed me. For turning my back on him, disregarding him, I felt the more I pushed myself in business, the more punishment I was enduring for the wrongdoings I believed I was guilty of.

Even though I didn't like you, I couldn't, wouldn't give you up. But your power was intoxicating. Your glamour reflected back to me in my mother's eyes. After introductions, the way Mom looked at you and carried on about me with you, I knew I had to keep you. Seeing Mom's pride and relief at my accomplishment, the joy of her beaming smile as she exhaled her fears and dreams into you, I accepted.

The affection and attention my mom showered me with made her image of me complete. I had become exactly what she sacrificed for me. What she gave of her life for, I did it; I had become it. The successful version of what she wanted for me, all of her hopes and dreams came to fruition at this moment. I owed it to her to be the way she wanted me to be. Secretly, I rejoiced in the pleasure that I was now a business owner, bigger, better, and more successful than she was. Somehow, this revenge was for my choice to comply with Mom, betraying myself in my youth. I took satisfaction in having the financial control over her now.

Inside Out, you offered me many benefits, but there was one particular remuneration that mattered to me more than all others, the crown jewel that I wore and would not give up, your protective shield, the armor I needed to survive. This was the disguise I was willing to give my life for. I gave everything I had to keep you: my health, my relationships, my heart. My dignity, my voice, and every resource I had, I gave to you in exchange for your protection.

You became the protection I needed as a five-, ten-, and fifteen-year-old girl, the little girl who looked different in this world. I felt terrified of standing out on my own in a world that seemed so cruel, a world that told me I was not wanted, was not welcomed, and didn't deserve a life here. I was told that I should be ashamed of myself for the choice my parents made to marry, to have me, a half-breed. I believed the world was willing to take me away from Mom, the only person in the world I trusted. The world told me it did not accept me, did not like me, and would not be bothered to see me destroyed.

The world told me that my half-black, half-white skin was shameful to the country. My skin was dirty; I was dirty for the sins of my parents. My skin was the outward appearance of the adults and authority figures; I was the dirty secret, secret shame of a society that didn't agree with the comingling of races. Until I washed myself clean of their disrespect to the black community and the white world, I was deemed wrong and bad, unworthy to have dreams and certainly not worth having those dreams come true. I believed the world would do me harm in school for not looking right. Adults told me and Mom that she was unfit to be a parent, an unfit mother deserving of punishment, of having her child removed from her care for her blatant disregard of the color lines. As a young child, I didn't know this was the way the world viewed me.

Inside Out, your image gave me protection from what I believed I needed protection from: people I thought wanted to hurt me, harm me, maliciously and intentionally want to cause harm to me. You protected me from them, from those who told me I was bad, wrong, inherently flawed, an abomination, and a sinner for the tone of my complexion. As a little girl, I didn't know to not believe them. I needed to keep my distance from everyone. Inside Out, you insulated me from all those who deemed me other.

The beliefs of few, I believed to be true, and created my world according to this belief. That I needed the image of you, of success for safety. That as long as you were big and mighty, you could and would protect me. Inside Out, you gave me the strength, power, and prestige I thought I needed to keep me out of harm's way.

Your image helped me feel and look strong. I had an aura of success; although a facade, you acted like a warrior, coming to my rescue whenever a threat seemed imminent. You gave me the false sense of security to stand alone and feel strong. Wielding my shield and warrior image, you became my external version of courage to the world, which I was unable to find internally on my own.

With you, I had the courage to fight any unwelcomed intruder, anyone I believed may be part of the coalition haunting me since I was a little girl. These people had been with me since I first understood the meaning of their disapproving glares. The evil in their hollow eyes told me to beware of their malicious intentions; I still feared them. People I didn't trust myself to identify or detect in society, I chose to assume everyone was willing to harm me for the color of my skin. In this way, I ensured I did not discern incorrectly and trust the wrong person. I felt some sense of control in my world that felt too big, too mean to control.

It was for this protection that I sacrificed my life for you, Inside Out. It was for this belief that you would do for me what I did not know how to do for myself, that I could not and would not let you go, even though you suffocated me. You consumed me by taking all I had: time, money, energy, and joy for life. I gave you everything, and you took all of it, strangulating me, leaving me gasping for life, until I had nothing left to give. Only in my despair and once you were gone could I accurately see you, see our relationship. As dysfunctional as it was, you were what I needed. You were of service to me, until I was ready. Until now. Now, I'm finally able to reconcile my mind. To make peace with my father, with my mother, the shackles that you bound me in began to loosen. I felt less and less in need of your protective image, needing to detangle the intertwined thread of us. I could detach from you, your false promises. As I began the arduous process of making amends to myself, to understand my life's choices, I had the clarity to see the misinterpretations I made as a child.

As I untangled myself from you, Inside Out, I saw that who I was, what I was, how I was is not in need of protection. Instead, I needed kindness, compassion for the little girl who didn't know what to do, how to protect herself, love and empathy for the little girl who was misinformed and made general assumptions that were inaccurate.

As the truth of my life became less ugly to me, less shameful, my need to keep my life, my past secrets hidden disintegrated. As my need to keep my secrets concealed for protection diminished, the need for you, Inside Out, paralleled. As the soft underbelly of my heart, my real self began to emerge as the strong being I am, the need to hide and protect myself from the perception the world would harm me weakened.

As the time has come to let you go, Inside Out, I must first thank you. Thank you for being my guardian, my provider, my protector. Thank you for taking care of me in the way you were able to, when I didn't know how to properly care for myself. Thank you for supporting me, allowing me to find character traits and qualities I knew I had, I just didn't know how to access them.

But most of all, thank you for knowing when it was time to leave me. Thank you, Inside Out, for knowing when it was time for me to go out into the world, unshielded, raw, open, exposed, and know I would be okay. Thank you for courageously stepping away, giving space for me to bloom and flourish and find my stable place on my own two feet. Thank you for pushing me out the door when I was too afraid to leave. Thank you for unveiling my gifts to me; for showing me my unique qualities, gifts, and talents as a healer; for bringing to my awareness the depths of my heart's yearning to contribute and be of service in the world. Thank you for your service, in revealing to me, reflecting back to me the misbeliefs I held, that were limiting my ability to fully express myself. Thank you for honoring my path, my journey, and giving me the space to find my way with dignity and love. Thank you.

EPILOGUE

Chapter 56

In the months following Mom's death, with time away from work, I gifted myself with space to heal. The process began with volleyball. Through the love, support of friends, I could feel my physical and emotional energy returning. Each day, while I missed Mom, I also felt free. Free to go through every drawer, cabinet, and cupboard, discerning which items to discard or keep, including the storage that had collected the remnants of Inside Out Wellness Center as well as Mom and my past lives in Northern California.

With each of Mom's items I let go of, I found myself becoming more and more free to step into the next chapter of my life. With each item of Inside Out I donated, I detangled myself from all the obligations of my past.

With each item released, a new life had room to emerge. A life I could now design as I chose. A life I could create for myself and Jasmine, based on my likes, my desires, my dreams. I felt free to give myself permission to ask and answer the questions, What do I want to do now?

The rage that once debilitated me is now gone. I am free. The terror that once consumed me has now subsided, giving way for me to find out more of who I really am and who am I becoming.

I have forgiven my mom, forgiven my dad, and most importantly, forgiven myself. I am finally at peace with my humanness, my human MESS.

With the courage to fully embrace that I am loved, I am loveable, I matter, and my life matters; the wounds in my heart finally healed.

"Until you heal the wounds of your past, you will continue to bleed. You can bandage the bleeding with food, with alcohol, with drugs, with work, with cigarettes, with sex, but eventually, it will all ooze through and stain your life. You must find the strength to open the wounds, stick your hands inside, pull out the core of the pain that is holding you in your past, the memories, and make peace with them."

"The truth will set you free, but first you must endure the labor pains of birthing it."

—*Iyanla Vanzant*

Final Note From The Author

It is my intention for this book to shower upon you, love and support as you travel through your process, discovering the depths of your soul and in becoming the grandest version of YOU.

You matter, Your life matters, You are loved and You are loveable,

With love, Natacha Nelson

"Out beyond ideas of wrong doing and right doing there is a field. I'll meet you there"

Rumi

Mom, Thank you

CPSIA information can be obtained
at www.ICGtesting.com
Printed in the USA
FFHW020712280319
51214761-56691FF